D0070997

Step
Back from the
EXIT

45 reasons to say **no** to suicide

Jillayne Arena

Copyright © 1995 by Jillayne Arena

Acknowledgments and permissions are located after the epilogue and form an extension of this copyright page.

All rights reserved. No part of this book may be reproduced in any form or by any means, electronic or mechanical, including photocopying, recording, or by any information storage and retrieval system, without permission in writing from the publisher.

Cover/Book Design: Jennifer Zehren
                       Montgomery Media, Inc.

Cover Photography: David R. Olson

The author of this book does not dispense medical advice nor prescribe any treatment without the advice of a professional. The author intends only to offer general information to help you cooperate with your health care professional in your mutual quest for health. In the event you use any information in this book for yourself, you are prescribing for yourself, which is your constitutional right, but the author and publisher assume no responsibility for your actions.

Library of Congress Catalog Card Number:
95–94711

ISBN: 0-9647340-0-1

Zebulon Press
P.O. Box 340788
Milwaukee, WI 53234

To
David, Joseph, and Carolyn

Thank You

To Carol, Don, Marilyn, Jean, Gladys, Deborah, Joni, and Denise for their comments and support.

To my husband's family. The Arena clan is a treasure of love and loyalty.

To the Milwaukee Public Library, its staff, and the hundreds of writers in their stacks who encouraged and inspired my journey.

To the Reader

Thank you for being with me while I was writing. Every time I turned on the computer, you were there. Without you, I wouldn't have written a line.

The suggestions in this book are not substitutes for professional advice. You deserve competent assistance with your specific needs; I pray you will find helpers and that you will work with them.

This book was written in bits, then loosely organized like a desk drawer: paper clips, bobby pins, and brass clasps in one bin, rubber bands, pony tail holders, and barrettes in another; duct tape and super glue are off to the side. Just open the book and rummage around until you find something you can use to hold yourself together.

contents

Preface xiii

1. It's Serious 1
When I consider my feelings seriously, others can too.

2. It's a Joke 3
When everything feels too serious, I need to look for the ironies and absurdities in my life.

3. Mister Rogers 5
People can like me just the way I am.

4. Finality 7
There are many experiences I could never have, including hugging my bear.

5. My Therapist 9
My death would make my therapist sad. If I can't imagine that, it's time to find a new therapist.

6. Chemistry 13
I might have a chemical imbalance that the right psychiatric drugs could make less severe.

7. Vitamins 17
I may have a vitamin deficiency.

8. Insomnia 21
Sleep deprivation is an ancient form of torture. If I haven't had a restful night, I shouldn't make irrevocable decisions.

9. Genes   23
There may be a genetic link to suicide.

10. Escape   27
Alcohol and other drugs can lower my inhibitions and allow my suicidal feelings to defeat me.

11. Courage   29
The world needs more, not fewer, people of determination and courage who have faced death and said, "not yet."

12. Perfectionism   31
To think the world would be perfect without me is perfectly ridiculous.

13. Control   33
Maybe I need to learn that I can't control everything.

14. Risk to Others   37
There is a risk I might kill a would-be rescuer, innocent bystander, friend, or family member in my attempt.

15. Funerals   41
Funerals are expensive.

16. I'm Not God   43
Suicide implies I know everything, but I'm not God.

17. Sin   45
Committing suicide is a sin and Hell might be worse than this.

18. The Devil   49
The devil can't make me do it, but he may be trying.

19. Being   51

I am a human being not a human doing.

20. Bad Manners   53

Committing suicide is like dropping in on God without an invitation.

21. Unseen Forces   55

Unseen forces, such as the moon's gravity or the length of sunshine in a day, may be affecting my mood.

22. Choices   57

Other choices exist, including making no choice at all.

23. Ghosts   61

I might end as a ghost in limbo, like Dickens' Jacob Marley, and have no recourse from my decision.

24. Regret   65

Those with near-death experiences after suicide attempts report regret for what they did and a renewed commitment to life.

25. Reincarnation   67

If there is reincarnation, I might have to come back and suffer this again.

26. Role Model   71

Whether I like it or not, I am a role model, who discourages and encourages others by my behavior.

27. My Children   73

Day care for my children is more expensive than therapy.

28. Friends 77
Suicide disturbs even casual acquaintances of the past and present.

29. My Husband 79
My husband could never find everything he needs to file the income taxes.

30. Love 81
Suicide denies me the opportunity to find out how much love is in the world and in myself.

31. Success 83
What if I die when I only meant to cry for help?

32. Failure 85
What if I live and severely disable myself when I wanted to die?

33. Law 87
Suicide is against the law and for good reason.

34. Shame on Me 91
Even a court should not decide if I deserve a death sentence for my behavior.

35. Shame on Them 93
Someone else's abusive behavior should not mean a death sentence for me.

36. Stories 95
Society, by definition, includes the stories of everyone, even the most despicable person: me.

37. Marilyn Monroe 99

Marilyn Monroe was glamorous; her suicide was not.

38. Heroism 101

Suicide denies me the chance to be my own hero, my own rescuer.

39. Magic 103

There may not be hope right now, but something magical or miraculous might happen any minute.

40. William Styron 105

Author William Styron is a hero to those who survive severe depression and suicidal thoughts.

41. Recovery 107

The highest priority is survival, not the overwhelming details of life.

42. E-motion 109

Sometimes what I do to make myself feel better makes me feel worse.

43. Gift 113

Although my life looks worthless now, I am curious to discover its worth.

44. Suffering 115

There is meaning in my suffering and I want to find it.

45. Truth and Lies 117

Suicide is a lie and cover-up. I want to learn the truth.

Epilogue 119

You cannot make yourself feel something you do not feel, but you can make yourself do right in spite of your feelings.
—Pearl S. Buck[1]

It is hard to say when I had my first suicidal thought. Was I a child, a high school student, or a college student? I cannot remember, but I know that by the time I started my first job after graduate school, suicidal thoughts were with me daily; gradually, relentlessly increasing in frequency until every minute they questioned my continuing existence.

Over the years, I responded to these thoughts in a variety of ways. I found some useful ways to cope (like taking vitamins), some useless strategies (like taking a bubble bath or restyling my hair), and some downright harmful responses (like drinking a tumbler of Chianti). Above all, I argued with myself, jawboned myself back from the edge, and kept the knives out of sight. As time dragged on and the assault of suicidal thoughts continued, my arguments grew into a whole litany of reasons for staying alive.

At one point during this struggle, I began writing down the arguments that helped me postpone my exit. Because the thoughts occurred over such a long period, I developed a long list. When one reason wasn't enough to hold back the black night, I would search for another and another, and the list would grow. The list became my flashlight, my amulet, my teddy bear.

If a reason could have changed my feelings, I wouldn't have needed a list. I cannot control my feelings, but my reasons helped me control my actions. They calmed me down, kept me going, and bought me the time I needed to reach out for help and to understand the feelings behind these thoughts.

Like Kevin in the movie *Home Alone*, I contended with the burglars by myself for many years. Why didn't Kevin call 911? Why didn't I get help sooner? I developed many excuses not to seek help, but it was more than denial or lack of willpower that kept me from seeking help. Like someone riding a Tilt-A-Whirl at the state fair, I was paralyzed, jammed up against the seat, unable even to blink because of the tremendous forces. At some point I moved my hand and dialed the phone. I still don't know how I did it.

Psychologists say that suicide is a permanent solution to a temporary problem, a forever decision. Well, that is easy to say but essentially meaningless to me. When the bottom of the blackness is dropping away, it is impossible to believe that a free fall into hell will end with a giant air bag. While in this dangerous, overwhelming position, I would ache for a permanent solution, crave doing something about my pain. Any solution now looked much better than any solution later, for I could see no bottom to this darkness. I thought I would fall forever. My feelings occur only in the present tense, and it's hard to imagine the future being anything but a permanent continuation of the present.

My feelings about the past, present, and future are my reality. They influence my thoughts and behavior. Does it help if someone says my feelings are temporary or even imaginary? I *know* my feelings are short-term, but I *feel* they are permanent. There are gaps between knowing and feeling as well as acting and feeling.

Some psychologists suggest that acting differently will change my feelings. Sure, following their advice changes the way I feel: I feel even more confused about my feelings! They make me think I can change, control, and distance myself from my feelings and I can't. They make me feel weak and ashamed because I can't turn down the noise from this lousy self-talk radio show. Yet, I can control my behavior. I do not have to act out or stamp out my feelings.

Freud talked of suicidal feelings as "murderous impulses against others redirected upon (the) self."[2] Today, psychologists speak of "anger turned inward." I am sure this idea is helpful to some. However, beyond verbal or physical or sexual violence, I had little idea of what anger really meant. Rage can hide behind many masks, including depression, anxiety, pain, feelings of emptiness, homelessness, fraudulence, and fatigue. If I could have felt my anger, Freud's idea might have made sense, but my rage was well hidden, and that was probably a good thing at the time. My anger was so deep, I could not let myself begin to feel it until I felt safer.

Anger was not the emotion I felt when sliding down the endless greasy pole. I felt withdrawn, numb, weak, guilty, afraid, stuck, and confused. Often, I could not feel anything, except the painful collapse of cells into some inner black hole. From within this collapse, it requires tremendous energy to reverse the momentum, and it has little to do with "murderous rage."

Others say time is the greatest ally. In whose war, I ask? Who could want more time in the middle of despair? I didn't think I could stand another minute or another day, or God help me, another year. That is the problem when outsiders look in: they simply cannot imagine the pain's density, its sucking vacuum, its lethal force, and so others respond with gestures akin to bandaging a compound fracture with a plastic strip.

If you see this book as such a gesture, that is OK. It has only one message and, although short, it is not simple: please step back from the exit.

Until that final door opens for each of us, there are lessons to learn, responsibilities to assume and let go, examples of fortitude to set, and humanity to express. Physical and mental abilities do not limit these experiences; there is no limit until after the last breath.

Step Back from the Exit

Here are my reasons for staying alive. Knowing that every day others find it impossible to imagine even one reason to postpone suicide, I reach out to you. This comes from my heart to yours on angel's wings. Please put together your own list so you also can step back.

one

It's Serious

The worst that can be said about him is that he runs the risk of being most humorous when he wishes to be most serious.
—Winston Churchill

When I consider my feelings seriously, others can too.

For years I would read those magazine articles touting "10 Ways to Beat the Blues," looking for the fairy-wand cure for my unhappy state. I couldn't admit that depression and suicidal thoughts are beyond "the blues." I can't conquer suicidal thoughts with an hour-long soak in an herbal bubble bath. As much as I want that to be true, it is not.

The articles would make me think that it was all so simple, yet I would feel worse after following the author's suggestions. They led me to believe I could get over this by relaxing, cutting down on stress, going on a vacation, sniffing flowers, drinking more milk, eating more pasta, doing something for someone else, getting some exercise, or taking up a new hobby.

When a weekend "away from it all" didn't chase away my blues, I used to feel even more anxious and upset because the vacation hadn't improved my outlook. After helping my elderly neighbor with grocery shopping so I could "stop feeling sorry for myself," I would also feel guilty because I felt worse, and worse yet, I did not know why. Trying behavioral changes didn't change my feelings except to increase my frustration and shame because I had somehow failed to beat my blues.

Actually, these activities took away the valuable energy I needed to understand that I had a problem. They bolstered my denial of the seriousness of my depression and wore me down further. By focusing on the first aid, I ignored the signs of gangrene and dangerously delayed seeking help until I was almost terminal. To think one could beat back suicidal thoughts with a good soak in the tub is a joke.

I worked with a former Marine who diffused bombs in booby-traps during the Vietnam War. Commonly, the enemy planted a bomb at the bottom of a camouflaged hole. A soldier on patrol would put his foot in the hole, and detonate the bomb as he removed his foot. If the soldier realized what was happening before taking his foot out, Mike could diffuse the bomb. Awed, I asked how he had survived.

He said, "I survived because I never took a break. Those who went for 'rest and recreation' on Okinawa inevitably came back and made a fatal mistake within the next day. I focused on my job and never let my guard down until I was on the plane home."

I can't take my survival for granted. If I take a break and go back to my myth that suicidal thoughts can be washed away in a hot tub, I risk losing the edge that is the key to my survival. I risk the craziness of trying to reconcile the easy solutions from the magazines with my deeply rooted feelings. If I don't give my suicidal feelings the serious attention and respect they deserve, I risk getting blown up.

two

It's a Joke

Comedy is an escape, not from truth but from despair; a narrow escape into faith.

—Christopher Fry[3]

When everything feels too serious, I need to look for the ironies and absurdities in my life.

OK, I need to lighten up. But who needs a trip to the Comedy Club, when so much material is so near? Tragedy is fertile ground for comedy. Perhaps the funniest people of our time, like Roseanne and John Belushi, developed their sense of humor as a foil to deep trauma or as a defense against hurt. Nobody develops a sense of humor who doesn't really need one for one reason or another. Like people who are blind using their other senses with greater acuity, those groping through life need to sharpen this sixth sense for daily survival.

I am not suggesting spending a weekend watching Marx Brothers movies. There is no worse insult than contrived cheering up. Someone took me to the circus right after my son was born to "cheer me up." I felt so miserable and misunderstood that I missed the joke. If I had been wiser, I would have taken a few lessons from the tightrope walkers, the clown who was shot out of a cannon, the lion tamer, and the ringmaster. Think what insights I could have learned from the sword swallowers, the knife throwers, the whip crackers, and the performing seals. Instead of sucking down blue raspberry slurpies, I should have been paying more attention to how the performers did their tricks. I could have saved years in therapy if only I had known how to run a circus.

It took me a long time before I could laugh at the ironies in various Christmas and birthday presents given my husband and me by one person over the years. These not-so-innocent presents have included: a sturdy brass letter opener, a pocket knife, soap-on-a-rope, glass tumblers, matches, scissors, surgical steel steak knives (a wedding gift), long scarves, a do-it-yourself guide to sharpening chisels, and, of course, new underwear. If this person wasn't so cheap, we would have received a real gun instead of the deluxe hot glue gun. What can we do but laugh?

Freud suggests that humor is a way for our unconscious to speak to us. He writes that humor allows "what is repressed to circumvent the resistances." We let repressed sensations into our conscious "temporarily...to the increase of our pleasure." [4]

Comic relief may offer more than momentary pleasure; it may be a way to receive new insights. When I heard myself joking about how consistently destructive the presents from this person were, I suddenly understood that person's real attitude toward me. Now I look forward to the gifts; they are always good for a secret laugh. Last year's Christmas present was a shoulder bag that hung down to my knees. A purse with such a long, stout strap was hard to find, I'm sure, but the laugh was worth it. It still makes me smile, although it went out with the wrapping paper.

Under excessive stress, insight is hard to come by. That is why therapy is an important tool for assembling life's bag full of unnumbered parts and why a good sense of humor is a prize. Through humor and insight, we can turn dreadful presents into genuine gifts. All seriousness aside, humor keeps us going when little else can.

(PS: Goodwill welcomes all gifts with underlying messages; donations may be tax deductible.)

three

Mister Rogers

It is a peculiar sensation, this double consciousness, this sense of always looking at one's self through the eyes of others.
—W. E. B. Du Bois[5]

There are people who can like me just the way I am.

It took many years before I could believe that anybody could like me just the way I am. I am not the only one who has had trouble with Mister Rogers. He is ripe material for comics because he tells a truth society has a tough time facing straight on. I call Fred Rogers my first therapist. Although our relationship was a little one-sided, I listened to him on *Mister Rogers' Neighborhood* since my children were little. He always says in closing: "You make each day a special day by just your being you. Remember, people can like you just the way you are."[6]

For my first five years of listening to this line, I had this inner argument: Oh, Fred, you never met me. God can't like me "just the way I am" — I learned that in Sunday School. What damnable pride to think I am special! I'm a sinfully wretched soul. How can you like me when I have no idea who I am? How dare you say that? It's practically blasphemy. People can't like me unless I share everything, love without conditions, forgive and forget injustice thoroughly, and "be good."

It finally came to me that if a guy like Mister Rogers could like me just the way I am, perhaps God's heart was big enough, too. Perhaps it was time to see my soul as having some intrinsic worth, created by a miracle rather than an accident. "Being good" instead of being me, I had spent thirty-five years as someone else. When Mister Rogers' message finally reached me, I took a first step toward accepting myself; my search could begin to find out who I really was. My life could start.

Now I know God loves me, and I am getting to like myself. From here, I can find people who like me just the way I am; people who like this mixed-up, messed-up, reclusive, and frightened person. Given time, I can find people who look past my puffy eyes, frown lines, and pasty cheeks into my heart. There are people who can help me find the soul that hid for years out of shame. I can find people who tell me by their actions that I make each day a special day just by being me.

four

Finality

Yes, I ask for a slow death and every possible infirmity. That is essential if I am to go without too much regret.

—Sacha Guitry

There are many experiences I could never have, including hugging my bear.

If I can't peer down from heaven or I get caught in the furnace below, I would never see my children smile again, or see them marry, have their own children, and live happily ever after. My tax refund check would arrive or the price of my stock would double, and I could never spend the proceeds. I would never feel the warmth of another human being or dog or cat again.

Yes, I imagine there are a thousand wonderful memories I could think about or a thousand experiences I could foresee. However, right now, I can't think. If I could leave this fog, I could remember rainbow endings to summer storms, collecting pretty rocks on a deserted beach, or lying on my back watching clouds that look like cotton candy.

If I could think, I could consider thousands of discoveries I have yet to make. I might discover a new friend, a new book, a new insight, a new song, or a new artist. Trying to think of pleasant thoughts, however, cannot erase the pain of now. However, playing a favorite piece of music or reading a favorite book might redirect the focus of my thoughts, at least temporarily.

My teddy bear is also an immediate comfort. Betty is a faithful, adorable brown bear. I named her after the mother of a grade-school friend who, on occasion, made an effort to make me feel special. At times, I have held on to life by the real Betty's silver thread of preciousness. My fuzzy Betty helps me remember her.

When I bought the bear, I joked with the manager that I must be the only big kid to come in and test bears for softhearted squashiness. With a dubious smile, he said, "People come in here all the time and hug the bears; that's my business."

Tomorrow, you could go to the store and pick out the softest, cuddliest, most kissable teddy bear. All right, tell them it's for your niece, if it makes you less anxious. Bring it home, think of a pleasing name for it, and then feel the warmth of the angels coming through the plush and button eyes.

A big, huggable bear is a twenty-four-hour friend and therapist. Splurge, indulge yourself with a high-quality stuffed animal. Beyond the initial investment, there is no upkeep. There are no veterinarian bills, no demands for dawn walks, no mouth to feed or water, just warmth on long, cold nights. To feel that warmth, it takes yielding the serious, easily embarrassed part of you to the part that needs a hug, the part that really wants to hold a warm teddy bear close to your heart. With a stuffed friend, you will find unconditional love and no fear of abandonment. Besides drinking warm milk in a loving mother's lap, hugging a bear under a soft quilt may be the most comforting activity known.

By temporarily relieving my pain, I put off an action that is final. If a small thought, action, or thread can pull me back one step from the exit, I have made a great stride toward recovery.

five

My Therapist

The unperturbed who feel the oldness—
All the sadness of the world—
Yet somehow feel the sacredness
Of grime upon the hands,
And even know the rush of pity
For the ones who know not
That some Power builds a callus out of blisters.
   — Carl Sandburg
      "To Whom My Hand Goes Out"[7]

**My death would make my therapist sad. If I can't imagine
that, it's time to find a new therapist.**

If you can't imagine one tear coming to your therapist's eye at
your death, it's time to find a new therapist. If you don't have
a therapist, now is the time to find one. I wanted to work my
feelings out alone, but I didn't get into this mess by myself,
and I need more than myself to get out of it. It is embarrassing to think of exposing our vulnerabilities to a stranger. The
plethora of "self-help" books reinforce the thinking that I can
and should get my stuff together by myself. Although, therapy
isn't something I want, it is something I need.

    Therapy is not a cure. As air circulates in and out of a
house, my feelings come from many places and interact in
many ways. For me, therapy is an opportunity to pull my

thoughts together, have someone witness my struggle, and gently guide me through my gopher maze of feelings. My weekly therapy session also provides me with a goal, even if it is short-term, as I dare myself to make it to my next appointment.

It bothers me to pick up a book or magazine article with a long section on "How to Choose a Therapist." They make it sound like researching a major appliance purchase or buying a used car. As I read their tips, the elaborate procedures suggested scare me off. It is easier to cook up excuses not to enter therapy than to follow the advice. One common pointer is to ask family, friends, and neighbors for references. Now, asking a friend for a reference would be quite an act of bravery for people already working their resolve overtime, and I admire anyone with the ability to do it. I can't even imagine asking my neighbor who her dentist is, although for most that is a straightforward request.

After collecting these references, the authors would have you screen the candidates over the phone. They tell you to ask questions about credentials, experience, techniques, specialties, policies, office hours, and price. Then they suggest you pare your list to two or three therapists to interview in person. If only I could be like those people who aren't too shy or tired to do all that checking and calling, I would tell myself, then I would find a therapist. After months of stewing, I finally figured out an easier way to find a good therapist.

My phone-phobic, low-energy scheme consists of two calls. The priority is to contact someone who has witnessed many therapists in action who can screen people for you. The person needed is an honest psychiatric nurse. To find one, call the switchboard of the local general hospital or psychiatric hospital. Speaking confidently (they can't see your hand shaking), ask them to connect you to the nursing station of the adult psychiatric unit (or adolescent unit or geriatric unit).

Tell the nurse you are looking for a therapist and need her/his most valuable advice in the matter. Ask for names. Nurses have seen many therapists' ethics, responsiveness, effectiveness, and humaneness. No amount of shopping and interviewing can substitute for their insight. If the nurse is reluctant, call another hospital or call during the next shift when a different nurse might not be as busy.

Why is it in their interest to give you names? First, it is the nurses who have to put you back together if you lose patience with yourself and try suicide. They would rather help you up front. Second, if they didn't care about patients, they could have better hours reviewing claims for an insurance company. That is phone call number one.

Now that you have some names and numbers, call one and make an appointment. Phone call number two may be more difficult, but you're halfway through. The hardest call I ever made was the initial call to my therapist. After I got his name, I put it off over a year! (OK, shame on me.) How about this: I dare you to call. If I could, I'd bribe you to call with a hot fudge sundae.

Breathe in slowly and deeply, then pick up the phone. Make the call. If this therapist is on vacation, doesn't return your call in a few hours, can't get you scheduled for three weeks, acts indisposed or indifferent, don't see it as personal or use it as an excuse. Perhaps this was not the person for you. Try someone else, right away, before you put your limited energy into denying the importance of your situation. After you have made the appointment, vow to keep it. Now, go get that sundae; you deserve a treat.

six

Chemistry

(When) you buy a pill and buy peace of mind with it, you get conditioned to cheap solutions instead of deep ones.

—Max Lerner[8]

I might have a chemical imbalance that the right psychiatric drugs could make less severe.

While many think space is the last frontier, what is between our ears is even more mysterious. The billions of cells in one brain easily outnumber the stars in the universe. These billions of cells communicate with chemicals in a complicated choreography scientists are only beginning to understand. When one chemical is scarce, present in the wrong amount or in the wrong place, humans can be in for emotional trouble.

Remember high school chemistry? Between poor measuring, dirty beakers, and the distracting boys at the next bench, none of my experiments came out. While I don't think of myself as much of a scientist, the work my brain cells accomplish in one second could win a Nobel Prize in chemistry. With what those cells have to work with, I'm sure they do the best they can, but sometimes they need a little professional help.

A physical checkup is a worthwhile investment. There could be a chemical or hormonal imbalance that the right drug could make less severe. It's worth considering. Currently hundreds of psychiatric drugs are on the market, five classes of antidepressants alone. As researchers find out more about the brain, new drugs seem to follow quickly. The newer drugs react more specifically and with fewer side effects, however, they are more expensive.

I have been on four different antidepressants in three years looking for a cure. At one point, I was sure I would have to try every drug on the market. The process of finding the right medication took so long that the drug I am on now was not even on the market when I started. Some early prescriptions I tried did more harm than good. "Trial and error" accurately describes the process my physician and I went through and "patient" is a good name for anyone involved with drug therapy.

While trying and erring, the psychiatric drugs became the focus of my frustrations. In my desperate search for an easy cure, the drugs held out a false hope. They dashed my spirits when I thought I was taking positive steps to get better. I found myself feeling worse, at times, in starting a new drug and building up an effective blood level. Drugs have been lifesavers for me, but they were not the cure I had hoped for. I am jealous of the vast majority of people for whom they work quickly and effectively.

Statistically, people do get better on antidepressants, especially when combined with talk therapy. Richard Restak writes in *The Mind:* "Even when satisfactory drugs are selected, administered in the correct dosage and are effective... most patients will benefit from concurrent psychotherapy."[9] He cites a major study at the National Institute of Mental Health called The Treatment of Depression Collaborative Research Program. Early in the study, researchers noticed the group receiving placebos clearly experienced a much slower recovery rate than those receiving drugs or therapy alone. Later studies in this program reinforce the effectiveness of drugs combined with talk.

For years, I wrote off my problems as a "chemical imbalance." I sought help for my suicidal feelings convinced everything was normal except my chemicals. It was disillusioning when, after several months, the pills had not cured me. The cold realization that I had work to do besides balancing my chemistry came with difficulty. According to Peter D. Kramer, in *Listening to Prozac,* "The message in the capsule is 'Dig here,' in physiology, as well as there ... in the territory of the mind." [10]

I am on a drug now that has few side effects for me. A friend was on the same drug for two weeks and claimed it turned her into a zombie. She's fine on a drug that almost sent me over the cliff. The point is that drug therapy is worth a try. However, I need to be patient while the doctor practices, and we both need to keep talking.

seven

Vitamins

Give me good digestion, Lord,
And also something to digest.
    —A Pilgrim's Grace

I may have a vitamin deficiency.

Vitamin deficiency diseases have been significant killers throughout history. Besides death, serious deficiencies of various vitamins can cause fatigue, confusion, depression, hallucinations, memory loss, and anxiety. Even less severe insufficiencies of vitamins, compounded by other factors such as protein deficiencies, alcohol or drug abuse or stress, could destroy our taste for life. Vitamins, minerals, and amino acids are chemicals necessary to maintaining healthy body tissues, including that big box of tissue perched on our necks.

Historically linked to madness, pellagra is one of many vitamin deficiency diseases. Before the discovery of niacin's involvement with pellagra, some scientists saw it as an inherited, fatal mental illness, while others saw it as a viral infection. Pellagra causes a variety of symptoms, including mental problems, depression, and episodes of mania. Around 1900, 10 percent of patients in state asylums in the southern United States were there because of pellagra.[11]

At that time, Joseph Goldberger, a U.S. Public Health Service doctor, observed that health care workers did not become infected with pellagra and that symptoms improved with diet.[12] With further work, he identified pellagra as a deficiency of the vitamin niacin, a scarce nutrient in the sharecroppers' diet of fatback, cornmeal, and molasses. A lack of the amino acid tryptophan, found in carbohydrates and made in the body from niacin, also can cause pellagra. A derivative of tryptophan, serotonin, is an important neuro-transmitter and plays a role in mood disorders.[13]

Joseph Goldberger's work resulted in the enforced fortifi-cation of milk and white flour that ended the high incidence of pellagra in the United States. However, today's common popcorn and low calorie soda regimen is not too far from the insane diet of times past. If a deficiency could land people in the asylum, an insufficiency might destabilize an already unstable person enough to want escape through suicide.

Two-time Nobel Prize-winning scientist Linus Pauling writes in his book, *How to Live Longer and Feel Better*, about anoth-er deficiency. He says that people with a deficiency in vitamin B_{12}, are likely to "become psychotic even before they become anemic." Mental disturbances, he found, "are also associated with deficiencies of vitamin C (depression), vitamin B_1 (depres-sion), vitamin B_6 (convulsions), folic acid, and biotin."[14] A deficiency of vitamin B_6 can also lead to depression because vitamin B_6 is also necessary for the metabolism of tryptophan. Because the B vitamins work together, taking large doses of one can throw the others out of balance and cause further harm.

Vegetarians, those who drink alcohol, take medications, smoke, are pregnant or nursing or growing rapidly— are all at risk for various deficiencies. An acquaintance on a macro-biotic diet was admitted to a psychiatric hospital after several days of hallucinations. When my friend went to visit her, she found her eating a roast beef sandwich. The nurses suggest-ed to her that she was not the first admitted after following a macrobiotic regimen and that the cure was in the cafeteria.

Beyond vitamins and amino acids, mineral imbalance also is suspect in causing nervous system disorders. Potassium, phosphorous, and calcium are involved in transmitting messages between neurons, while magnesium and chromium are involved in regulating blood sugar and the production of glucose, the energy the brain uses.

When I was using birth control pills, I was convinced the pills were causing a deficiency that caused my depression. Wouldn't that have been easy? I tried to follow a diet recommended in a book, but gave up shortly in favor of vitamin pills. The supplements I began taking helped me feel better, but didn't eliminate the depression. Yet, in recognizing my depression and my need for vitamins, I made a respectable start on my long and twisting journey.

Of course, we're not helping ourselves by eating a poor diet. When we're down, who has the energy to cook and shop for food, let alone the desire to eat it? I confess to living on cookies and microwave TV dinners for years. Most nutritional labeling only confirms the void in food, but a good place to start comparing labels is the bread aisle. If you eliminate all bread in white wrappers, there aren't many left to check, and the comparison is surprising. While white bread contains the government-mandated minimum fortification, whole grain breads are a good source of protein, other B vitamins, vitamin E and minerals. Eating a good-tasting, nutritious bread at least puts the bottom on our food pyramid.

If you can't drag yourself through the 3,000 items in the average grocery store, find the energy to ask a pharmacist for advice on what vitamin or mineral supplements you might need. If you have more energy than that, talk to a doctor or nutritionist or read a reliable book. However, beware of those who would tell you it's only a matter of eating better. When you feel better, you can make better food choices and eat more nutritiously, but feeling better has to come first.

Taking vitamins was not a cure for me. By taking vitamins, however, I could rule out their deficiency as a cause of my poor mental state. The insane, institutionalized pellagra victims of the early 1900s would not have hesitated to call vitamins a cure.

eight

Insomnia

And even in our sleep, pain that cannot forget falls drop by drop upon the heart, and in our despair, against our will, comes wisdom to us by the awful grace of God.

—Aeschylus

Sleep deprivation is an ancient form of torture. If I haven't had a restful night, I shouldn't make irrevocable decisions.

I can't end my life forever just to get one good night's sleep. If I haven't had a good night's sleep in some time, all the better reason to get a good night's sleep and then decide. I have been waiting ten years for that good night's sleep. Maybe it will come tonight.

Under the heading of insomnia, there is a variety of sleeplessness. Some people have a hard time falling asleep while others wake up several times during the night. Others wake up too early in the morning. There are also people like me who have trouble falling asleep, wake several times each night, and wake too early. Others don't have insomnia at all but sleep too much and still feel tired. Anyhow, tackling a day without a refreshing night's sleep feels like trudging through a blizzard.

There are a variety of factors that can trigger insomnia. Besides depression and anxiety, illnesses such as Parkinson's disease, Alzheimer's, sleep apnea, heart disease, diabetes, asthma, ulcers, and sinus trouble can cause insomnia. In addition, smoking, alcohol, caffeine, medications, and drug interactions can interfere with sleep.[15]

Gerald Snyder writes in *Useful Information on Sleep Disorders*: "With rare exceptions, insomnia is a symptom of a problem, and not the problem itself. Good sleep is a sign of health. Poor sleep is often a sign of some malfunctioning and may signal either minor or serious medical or psychiatric disorders."[16] Researchers are still trying to figure out if insomnia causes depression or if depression causes insomnia.[17] Probably, there is truth in both statements. Checking out the cause of sleeplessness with a physician may prevent further complications.

What would I give for a good night's sleep? When will the sleepless nights and dragged-down days end? Sometimes I want to induce permanent sleep when eight hours of escape into sweet dreams would do perfectly. The injustice of needing sleep so desperately, and yet being unable to get it, is hard to endure. Yet, grudgingly each morning, I pull on my waders and start the slog through today's swamps. Perhaps tomorrow I'll find solid ground. Wrestling with life on a poor night's sleep is difficult at best and unbearable torture at worst. Still, tonight may be the night sleep comes.

nine

Genes

Science is a first-rate piece of furniture for a man's upper chamber, if he has common sense on the ground floor.

—Oliver Wendell Holmes[18]

There may be a genetic link to suicide.

My great-grandfather ended his life by drinking an agricultural chemical and a great-uncle drank himself to death with alcohol. Is suicide part of my genetic heritage, or is there a heritage of dysfunction, or is this a coincidence? Research in this area is advancing rapidly with the development of new technologies, but the current human genome map is more like a sketch for finding Captain Hook's treasure than a detailed street guide.

If scientists find a genetic link in mood and impulse disorders, there might be some sort of intervention available in the future. After researchers test genetic theories and find specific defects, they can develop gene replacement therapies or pharmaceuticals targeted to specific deficiencies in hormones, neurotransmitters, or pain and pleasure receptors. Gene therapy for treating cystic fibrosis is already in the clinical trial stage and others are not far off.

Inheritance, however, is not solely genetic. Child abuse and family violence can be legacies passed down from one generation to another through behavior modeling.

Behavior modeling, environmental factors, and genes all have a role to play in mood disorders and suicide, although the role of each is not clear.

Ernest Hemingway, his brother, and father all killed themselves violently. The three also drank heavily and suffered from depression. Is the genetic link in the alcohol abuse, the depression, the violence, or suicide, specifically? How do scientists account for behavior modeling and environmental factors in studying family tendencies? Are these factors a consequence or a cause?

Many genes could be involved as opposed to one particular culprit. With a genetic lack of gastric acid, poor metabolism of vitamin B_{12} results. Without this vitamin, pernicious anemia sets in and causes fatigue, memory loss, and depression.[19] One could hardly call it a gene for depression, but depression is one result of this genetic defect. A genetic predisposition to unusually low serum cholesterol might result in lower brain-cell-membrane cholesterol. This might result in poor serotonin uptake that might result in suicidal tendencies.[20] Is this a gene for suicide? Research is only beginning to show how much more there is left to find out.

Studies of identical twins show some interesting results. If one twin suffers a depressive disorder, the other twin has a 50 percent chance of also having a disorder.[21] The rate for identical twins reared apart is similar. On the other hand, fraternal twins have only a 10 percent chance of both suffering from a depressive disorder. Another twin study concluded that "the estimated heritability of depressive symptoms was between 30 and 37 percent."[22] Genes play a role, but are apparently not absolute determiners of illness.

Scientists at the University of North Carolina School of Medicine in Chapel Hill are studying a gene that may be a predisposing factor in up to 8 percent of all suicides and psychiatric hospitalizations in the United States.[23] The gene causes Wolfram syndrome, a disease characterized by diabetes, severe vision disturbances, and neurological disorders. Further research is necessary to isolate this gene, identify its physiological impact, and develop intervention strategies.

Future studies will, undoubtedly, find more clues to deciphering the effect of genes on moods and feelings. Until then, maybe I can help the future along by volunteering at a medical college or hospital for a study. Who knows what they would find in a spot of my DNA? Alien blood? Primordial ooze? Biology, however, is not my entire destiny, although I may have to negotiate with it. Until science has the upper hand, I'll keep the cork in the bottle and let the dandelions go.

ten

Escape

They speak of my drinking, but never think of my thirst.
 —Scottish Proverb

Alcohol and other drugs can lower my inhibitions and allow my suicidal feelings to defeat me.

A strong correlation between alcohol abuse and drug abuse with suicide is clear. According to Frank Crumley, "Psychoactive substance abuse appears to be associated with a greater frequency and repetitiveness of suicide attempts, more medically lethal attempts, a measured seriousness of intention, and greater suicidal ideation."[24] It is not difficult to see that excessive drinking and taking illegal drugs are suicidal acts in themselves.

Alcohol lessens our ability to control our behavior and restrain the expression of our emotions. Alcohol is a known depressant. After an initial high, alcohol negatively alters our mood. For those in pain and under stress, it is quick, available, and inexpensive relief. Combining these factors, it doesn't require a million-dollar grant to figure out why alcohol and suicidal thoughts feed on each other, and then consume us.

Self-medicating depression with alcohol probably goes back as far as 4000 BC with the beginning of brewing in Babylon. Well before 1000 BC, the philosopher of Ecclesiastes wrote, "I decided to cheer myself up with wine and have a good time." (Eccles. 2.3 TEV) It has been the drug of choice for millennia.

Applying our twentieth-century knowledge of physiology, however, we know that alcohol's relief is temporary. We drink to relieve pain, but pain relief is temporary. After the initial relief, we are more depressed and crave more relief. Worse off than when we started, the abusive spiral begins. The depressive action of alcohol and the disillusionment of temporary relief set us up for more drinking, mood swings, and more lethal suicidal behavior.

Unfortunately, alcohol and drugs give some the mettle to commit suicide. For others, drugs numb the pain enough to help them make it through the day. Neither is a solution. The point is to straighten ourselves out enough so we can stop focusing on escape and start focusing on what it is we cannot face.

Breaking the cycle of seeking temporary relief for our underlying despair is difficult. Dr. Richard Miller, a drug treatment program director, feels those with compulsive behavior share a similar trait — "the unwillingness on the part of the human being to confront and be with his or her human feelings."[25]

We need to seek lasting relief, not by committing suicide or drinking, but by working on the issues prompting our need to escape. Can we find the fortitude in the deepest part of ourselves or can we find it in a Higher Power? I'm sure we would all agree that courage doesn't come from a bottle. Instead, we need to reach inside for courage and reach out to those who can help us.

eleven

Courage

'Tisn't life that matters!
'Tis the courage you bring to it.
        —Hugh Walpole[26]

The world needs more, not fewer, people of determination and courage who have faced death and said, "not yet."

The world's most courageous people are those who have every reason to want death but have said, "not yet." It is difficult to look past the negative examples set in our society today and mentally counter the messages of those who insist others have a right (or obligation) to die. In the natural world, suicide is rare. Occasionally, a heartsick dog might refuse food, but he wouldn't deliberately run into a car. *Doggedness* means tenacity. In nature, there are abundant examples of determination and perseverance.

One spring day, I picked up a winter's accumulation of litter in a nearby cul-de-sac. Surprisingly, on top of discarded plastic bags, I found little worlds of sprouts and slugs in the decaying leaves. In another place, I saw that a shoot had split a foam coffee cup and was shredding the suffocating material with all its strength. For all the junk food litter, shattered glass, and soft drink cans, nature persisted. Even if I hadn't removed the human debris, nature's stubbornness would be clear by midsummer.

On a larger scale, the earth is under siege. Daily newscasts describe crises in the rain forests, oceans, and upper atmosphere. Despite the bleak picture, the planet hasn't given up in one cosmic explosion. There are signs of hope. Two decades ago, they joked about walking on Lake Erie, or at least burning it; it was dying. Today, it is alive with activity. Nature's fierce determination to survive, given the smallest sliver of hope is an inspiration. The planet continues to renew itself despite our abuse. Yet, the earth needs our tenacity too. Lake Erie renewed itself because determined people gave the lake a second chance. The earth needs more tenacious people to help it recover, yet the earth itself sets a powerful example of renewal.

If there aren't examples of hope in people, there are plenty in nature. Appearing to die in the fall, trees bud again in spring. Depression is the soul's "winter of discontent," its frozen state of suspended animation. In time, the bears and bees come out of hibernation, ready for a new season of life. In nature's cycles and seasons, there is hope. Let's find in nature's determination our own determination. Maybe nature is the teacher, and perseverance is our lesson.

When a seriously ill person commits suicide, it discourages others who try to keep going. Suicide denies us their example of determination. Even with intellect or mobility reduced, people can still show determination, fortitude and dignity by not giving up. The elderly who give up in the face of adversity send a confused message to the young people who can renew our world and breathe fresh solutions into the seemingly insurmountable problems we have created. Is suicide the only lesson the terminally ill can teach us? Is suicide the only response to chronic pain, Alzheimer's disease, or advanced cancer? These elders do not speak with the authority of our oldest mother, Mother Nature. When it seems humanity is failing, nature doggedly, bullishly, mulishly exerts her right to exist. We need nature, but nature needs us too.

twelve

Perfectionism

Sacrificers are not the ones to pity; the ones to pity are those they sacrifice.
—Elizabeth Bowen[27]

To think the world would be perfect without me is perfectly ridiculous.

My human nature desperately needs to preserve the Myth of the Perfect Family. I am all too willing to direct this charade. My family is all too willing to support this effort. I want to imagine I had a happy childhood, even if I can't let myself remember it. Wasn't it like *Leave It to Beaver* or *The Brady Bunch*? Didn't we work out our problems with great love and respect in only twenty-three minutes?

More likely, the repeated admonition, "Now, you be good" characterizes my childhood. That phrase was usually followed with the question: "Can't you see you're driving me crazy?" Having heard these repeated several hundred times, is it a wonder I believe I am to blame for everything? My child mind thought: if I am good, the craziness will stop; the craziness results from my imperfection; if I can't see that the craziness is my fault, then obviously I am not good enough. What a myth!

I sought professional help because I thought I was the sick one, and my cure would make everything perfect again. While I work at making my life less crazy, family members focus their unhappiness on me and my problems, desperately fighting to preserve their own idealized version of reality.

In their view, everything would be perfect if I got a job like Buffy, had married a man like Duke, permed my hair like Babs, and wore a more becoming shade of lipstick. Worse, they believe that everything would be better if I took a different antidepressant, worked harder at therapy, found a different therapist, or ended therapy altogether. A voice from childhood calls out, "Don't forget to haul out the trash!" Am I responsible for taking out all of the garbage?

More dangerously, in being conditioned to agree with this thinking, I extend their logic, believing everything would be perfect if I were dead. When it becomes dangerous to my life, I must no longer deny that my whole perfect family is sick. This is no longer a matter of playing the family scape-goat; it is a matter of life and death. Suicide is a martyring to redeem the Perfect Family Myth; if I die, then everything will be perfect. Suicide is a human sacrifice to the myth's god.

Debunking the myth requires strength; it is easier to think otherwise. Anne Wilson Schaef writes in *Co-Dependence: Misunderstood—Mistreated* that martyrs think their sacrifice is for a just cause like keeping the family together or hiding socially unacceptable behavior. The martyr's "belief in the importance of suffering just helps perpetuate a destructive situation."[28] Suicide looks like a viable solution to those exhausted from failing to keep all of life's plates spinning at once, and it preserves the myth.

Challenging the myth of my family may be the most difficult task of my lifetime. Hard as the task is, the price of maintaining the myth is too high. I am not a foreign agent on a mission for the Mother Country, sworn to swallow the cyanide capsule if ever put in a situation that would dishonor Her Majesty the Queen. I am not a savior, bearing everyone's sins on my cross. I am not perfect, but I am not Jesus or James Bond either. Martyring myself to save a myth accomplishes little except my destruction.

thirteen

Control

Life is to be lived, not controlled, and humanity is won by continuing to play in the face of certain defeat.
—Ralph Ellison[29]

Perhaps I need to learn that I can't control everything.

Suicide's temptation is control, yet suicidal thoughts have been almost impossible for me to control. The thoughts come at midnight while I lie in bed next to the red glow of the digital clock; they come as nightmares in dreams that should be healing escapes; they come while I walk along a Lake Michigan beach engrossed in the infinite patterns made by waves and beach gravel. I have tried taming them with logic, hot fudge, Mozart, Xanax, stair-climbing, and yoga; still, they come. As much as I would like the power, my own feelings, and other's thoughts and actions are outside my control.

Commercials promote the illusion that I can control and influence other people's opinions and actions by using the right breath mint, deodorant, cake mix, floral arrangement, or blue jeans. Advertisers manipulate images and symbols, sell "sizzle, not steak," and turn passing fancies into got-to-have-it needs. Advertisers view a lack of "sales response" as a failed ad campaign. I want to believe that given the right words, music, and video, I can direct the behavior of others. Then, if I can't, I blame my poor marketing skills. Yet, long-stemmed roses, hot clothes, or double chocolate brownies can't make another person stop emotionally abusing me, quit drinking, or get a decent job.

Although I like to fantasize that I have everything and everybody under my control, do I want the responsibility that would go with that power? I may want the power to convince someone to go to Alcoholics Anonymous meetings, to persuade my friend to go back to college, to influence your behavior with this book, but these decisions should be beyond my control. One life is enough to live at a time. If I had power over others, responsibility would go with it, and I am not sure I want the follow-up. What I really want is the power of a two-year-old who has learned to say "no" in rhythm with a spoon banging on a highchair, or who knows whining long enough will bring a cookie.

Attempting to control the uncontrollable is like lassoing a hurricane. Although it doesn't prevent me from trying to imitate Pecos Bill, I do not have to accept lack of controlling the impossible as failure. It's tough to let go of controlling these thoughts and yet not become their victim. Engaging in all kinds of therapeutic activities might lead me to a solution; still, I cannot entirely control my progress. I might have to wait until the hurricane dissolves itself.

Popular self-improvement books would have me "making friends" with my disintegrated state of mind, "embracing" it, and being "grateful" for it. Well, depression and suicidal thoughts are no friends of mine, but I will not deny having learned an untold amount from my experience. I am grateful for the insights depression has given me, but in trying to "possess my disease," I delude myself into thinking I am in control. Worse yet, I feel I have failed because I am too weak to get rid of my affliction, or that I am not getting better because I am "holding onto" my disease for some other sick reason.

In searching for the middle ground between controlling and being controlled, I wrestle between the roles of hapless victim and all-knowing god. Like riding a bicycle, I cannot change the facts of gravity and physics, but in acknowledging their presence, I can move forward, free within their boundaries. I can control my speed and direction, anticipate the actions of others and change my course, compensate for the environment, wear a helmet, and go with the flow. The alternative is landing on my face.

fourteen

Risk to Others

The web of life is like a spider's web: touch any part and the entire web shimmers.

—Joseph Sittler

There is a risk I might kill a would-be rescuer, innocent bystander, friend, or family member in my attempt.

"Fumes kill 3 at home of WISN-TV official,"[30] the headline announced. Police and witnesses speculated that the wife of a local media executive had walked into her garage and locked the door behind herself sometime around midnight. Wearing only her nightgown, she had slipped behind the wheel of her Continental and turned on the ignition.

According to reports, the car's gas tank was found empty and carbon monoxide had filled the garage, the caretaker's apartment above the garage, and the main living areas of the house. As the fumes seeped into the apartment, my friend Jim slept, never to wake. Two others were in the house; one, her husband, recovered.

Jim mentored me on my first job after graduate school. I cried in his office one day at the bank where we worked, and I still remember the smell of starch in the fresh linen handkerchief he handed me. Later, when Jim explained to me that the doors in the Personnel Department had special hinges allowing them to swing both ways, we laughed so hard the tears came again. I remember drinking coffee with Jim and reading the employment section of the *Wall Street Journal*. How we laughed as we cruised the Swiss-cheese-looking classified ads; others were looking elsewhere too.

Jim shook my hand and congratulated me the day I left the bank. Not many did. As he pressed his hand in mine, he said, "Good luck on that new job. Of course, you'll do well, whatever you try."

"I'm not much of a banker," I said. "Then again, maybe I didn't try. Thanks for everything."

He leaned close and smiled. "Let me know if they have any other openings at your new job."

That was the last time I saw Jim alive. Now his story reminds me that I live in a web, not on an island. I see those headlines again when life feels too long, too hard, too much. I hear Jim's words of comfort and encouragement. I smell a newspaper's fresh ink and the scorched aroma of vending-machine coffee in fragile paper cups.

Suicide was her choice, but it wasn't Jim's choice or the choice of his house guest. I'm sure she had no intention of hurting anyone, but she did and her death caused the deaths of two others. In turn, these deaths affected families, friends, the community, and me.

I didn't want to believe how interconnected we all are, but she showed me that connection dramatically. Like the early A-bomb testers, I wanted to believe that there are remote Pacific islands that can disappear into the wide ocean without a ripple. Yet, bomb tests have changed the ocean's ecology at those sites. No matter how isolated I feel, I exist within a society; I am part of an ecosystem.

Ann Landers once published a letter from a distraught mother whose daughter died while walking down the street. A man had crushed her after jumping from a skyscraper. Joseph Campbell tells a story about two Hawaiian police officers who came upon a young man ready to jump from a cliff. With no thought for his own life, the first officer grabbed the man and caught him as he jumped. As he was pulled down, the second officer arrived in time to pull them both back. The officers insisted that reaching out was an automatic human response. "Our true reality," Campbell writes, "is in our identity and unity with all life. For it is, according to Schopenhauer, the truth of your life."[31]

In disconnecting myself from the web of life, I run the risk of disconnecting others. Even if I can't live for myself, I can't face the possibility of accidentally depriving other people of life by my choice.

fifteen

Funerals

*Over the years the funeral men have constructed their own grotesque
cloud-cuckooland where the trappings of Gracious Living are trans-
formed, as in a nightmare, into the trappings of Gracious Dying.*
—Jessica Mitford[32]

Funerals are expensive.

Despite suicidal thoughts, I am still practical. Think of what
therapy costs and then how much funerals cost; there is no
comparison. I value a dollar as much as anyone and don't
wish to throw it in the ground. Even when therapy seems a
waste, at least it's spending on something living. There is a
potential return on that investment, although it may not pay
out as quickly as I would like.

I have contemplated a simple funeral in the chapel of the
local cemetery. Yet doing this ceremony as cheaply as possible
is still expensive. A basic corrugated fiberboard coffin is $280.
Borrowing a van to carry the box to the crematorium would
save some money. Cremation itself would run around $200;
with an additional ten-dollar plastic urn and carnations from
the grocery store, it would cost a minimum of $500 to dispose
of my body. However, even if my family followed my wishes,
they wouldn't find these deals without a lot of shopping.

Probably, my family wouldn't settle for such a bargain-
priced affair. A funeral would probably set them back ten

times the amount of the simple cremation. The average funeral cost $4,077 in 1994, according to the National Funeral Directors Association in Milwaukee, Wisconsin. That figure included an 18-gauge steel, velvet-lined casket and the services of a funeral home, but did not include burial, monument, vault, or plot. Purchasing a finer copper casket with metal handles alone would cost over $4,000.

A plot in a cemetery in Milwaukee, Wisconsin starts at about $300, with grave-digging services about $400 extra. I wouldn't like to price it in New York City. However, it would cost close to $1,000 to fly the body from New York to Milwaukee, if one shops for discounts.

Without much looking around, I can find individual and group therapy that costs far less money than a funeral. Insurance or government payments could stretch that money for years with the money that could have gone for funeral expenses. But, if sticking my survivors with a large bill is what I want, it might be better to sue them to pay for therapy. That would get some attention. Of course, funeral directors are more than willing to help with preplanning and prepaying and personal injury attorneys are more than willing to discuss lawsuits, but a caring therapist might have my better interests in mind.

sixteen

I'm Not God

All power is sacred power because it begins in the hunger for immortality.
—Ernest Becker[33]

Suicide implies that I know everything, but I'm not God.

My reality is that I am not omniscient. Even with the advice of experts, I cannot reliably predict the future or know every detail of the present or past. If the meteorologists issue a thunderstorm watch, will it really storm over my house? When pollsters predict the results of an election, many do not show up to vote and that can change the election's result. Historians have difficulty describing the past, too. They think they have the facts interpreted accurately until some general's granddaughter finds a trunk filled with her grandpa's letters in her attic. As a community, the view is not clear; as an individual, the view is thickly frosted.

When I began to write down my reasons for living, I did not know I would have so many they would turn into a manuscript. When it occurred to me that there were enough reasons to fill a book, I thought that the first publisher I contacted would pay me an advance for my scratchy outline and then take care of everything. That was a pleasant fantasy, but after the rejections got into the double digits, I knew I had work to do. I reminded myself that I was not writing for agents and publishers, I was writing for people like myself who need one good reason to get through the next ten minutes. How this book will turn out is a mystery, but I have gotten beyond the easy fantasy into faith; faith that if I do my best work, God (the Universe, the Fates, destiny) will take care of the rest.

Often, faith comes with the adjective "blind." Beyond my limited scope, I am blind to present and future possibilities, but in faith I continue stringing words together, taking writing classes, and revising. Someday I will see the finished book. Someday the present will be history, but even that will not be entirely clear. One lesson is clear: I am not God.

Somehow though, I am a part of God, a part of the Universe, a dot on an "i" in a word I don't know, in a thought I am not privy to. I will not know what part I play unless I stay around to find out. The present is a question mark, a semicolon, a comma, but not a period.

Life presents apparently insurmountable challenges, yet I can only speculate on the outcome, guessing at my ability to handle the future I predict. However, that may not be the future at all. I make the dangerous presumption that the Great Jill knows all and sees all. Thankfully, I have been wrong. Life reveals itself minute by minute. In presuming I am too weak to meet the future, I presume the enemy has me outnumbered, and I do not know that for sure. By acknowledging the limits of my awareness, I find the greater vision of faith.

seventeen

Sin

There is but one thing more dangerous than sin—the murder of a man's sense of sin.
　　—Pope John Paul II [34]

Committing suicide is a sin and Hell might be worse than this.

The theological issue of suicide has been studied for millennia. Plato (c.428-348 BC) writes: "Man is a prisoner who has no right to open the door of his prison and run away.... A man should wait, and not take his own life until God summons him."[35]

Saint Thomas Aquinas (c.1225-1274) argued in his *Summa Theologica* that suicide is a sin against God. He reasoned that suicide is contrary to nature as every organism naturally wants to preserve its life. Further, it is contrary to social obligations because self-killing injures the whole human community. Finally, he said that it is contrary to religion in that God alone should decide when a person will die.

Aquinas writes: "To bring death upon oneself in order to escape the other afflictions of this life is to adopt a greater evil in order to avoid a lesser. Suicide is the most fatal of sins because it cannot be repented of."[36]

Immanuel Kant, writing in the late eighteenth century, also used theology to reject suicide. He writes: "As soon as we examine suicide from the standpoint of religion we immediately see it in its true light."[37]

Twentieth-century Lutheran theologian Dietrich Bonhoeffer writes in his *Ethics* that God should decide the timing of our death "because He alone knows the goal to which it is His will to lead it." Before Hitler had him executed for participating in the German resistance, Bonhoeffer wrote: "Even if his earthly life has become a torment for him, he must commit it intact into God's hand, from which it came, and he must not try to break free by his own efforts, for in dying he falls again into the hand of God, which he found too severe while he lived."[38]

New thinking in medical ethics has blurred many theological arguments. Theology is dismissed by some as an "external source," thereby making these arguments "unconvincing." So the problem is in finding out the "person's deepest autonomous wishes, including his or her hopes for the future." The desire for suicide can come from a wish for self-punishment, a need to communicate, a wish to help when terminally ill, or fear of an unknown and possibly painful future. Underneath, however, at the molten-iron depth of my core, there is a desire for life. "Surface intentions do not always capture deeper desires or inclinations, and in a matter as serious as suicide deeper motives should receive a heavy weighting."[39] When I am so confused, neither external nor internal arguments make sense, but I do think about Hell.

Despite the historical sanctions against "running away from my prison," and the chance Dante's Inferno is real, sometimes Hell looks like an improvement on where I am right now. Sometimes Hell looks like a relief. There, at least, people can "weep and gnash their teeth." I envy those who know how to cry out their sorrow and bitterness; my tears are stuck somewhere. Sometimes I am jealous that people in

Hell seem to have an outlet for pain in tears, however, they never stop crying. They have no course of action open to resolve their pain as they had on earth.

Those in Hell have no expectations. At least Hell's prisoners must concede to their situation. Here on earth, the Carrot of Hope dangles in front of me, trying to entice me with tomorrow. Tomorrow might be the day when my dark mood will lift, when my pain will cease, when relief will come. Often, however, I am unable to see any chance for improvement, any possibility for new solutions.

Hope implies that something desirable is obtainable. Like a cat jumping and clawing at a fake mouse that someone continually yanks out of reach, I feel teased and tortured. Just when I am ready to give up, the dangler lets me touch the toy for a second, and I renew my pursuit. Hell's souls don't have that torture. Not for a minute can they believe anything can change.

Considering the arguments, I have decided to bet my life that an inferno exists. I wager that the odds are that despite my prison, Hell is worse. I would rather not find out if I am right or wrong. It is a one-way ticket. There is no peeking; no time to look the landscape over and come back. There is no opportunity to repent, but an eternity for regret. Worst of all, my fellow demons might be the people or problems I am trying to avoid in this life. An eternity with them would be Hell!

eighteen

The Devil

The evil of the world is made possible by nothing but the sanction you give it.

—Ayn Rand[40]

The devil can't make me do it, but he may be trying.

Some people believe in the goodness of everything, or that everything is benignly neutral, neither good nor bad. I believe, however, that evil exists and that the spirit of the devil is found in many forms. "Evil" spelled backward is "live," and the devil is involved with all things counter to life.

At times, I feel the devil-spirit harassing the better part of my nature, wearing infinite disguises, using people and events to confuse me, planting thoughts in my head. It is the evil one speaking the suicidal thoughts, and identifying the speaker helps me separate this voice from mine. While the devil pesters me with suicidal thoughts, I stubbornly reject his taunting and ask the angels to protect me. The Hebrew name for the devil, Beelzebub, means "Lord of the Flies," and more specifically flies as pests rather than flies as insects.

This teasing spirit wears me down until I would like to give in just to get rid of it. In the struggle between good and evil, giving in to evil seems easier than fighting, but giving in only makes evil stronger. Giving in to evil makes it easier for the devil to conquer others. Yet in this struggle, there are allies.

The *Star Wars* movie trilogy powerfully portrays the struggle between good and evil. In these movies, the noble young hero, Luke Skywalker, battles the dark forces of the Evil Empire. Luke, however, does not struggle alone; he uses his light saber, a symbol of the Force. His teacher, Ben Kenobi, tells Luke, "The Force is an energy field created by all living things. It surrounds us, it penetrates us, it binds the galaxy together." Like Luke, to succeed in my battle against the devil's evil thoughts, I must call on the Force and feel its power within me.

For many years, my beliefs were confused, and I have come to understand that confusion is the hallmark of the devil. Growing up in a parsonage, thirty feet from the church door, I thought of God as a patrol officer tailing me twenty-four hours a day. At the gates of heaven, I thought I would find a stack of tickets for seemingly horrendous offenses such as dribbling chocolate milk, using my dessert fork for a salad, interrupting conversations, and incorrectly trimming my toenails. I was sure God judged my thoughts before I could think them, so I tried hard not to think.

It was the devil that kept me from feeling God's love. God is a force for life and not a crotchety nitpicker. Yet I still struggle, fighting lies, confusion, ugliness, and pretensions in myself. In this struggle, I need to remember that I don't have to fight evil alone; help is available. Carl Jung would call the dark side within me the "shadow self," but it feels better to think of evil as alien, to think my core, my soul is good and without intrinsic shadows. In learning to recognize the shadows, however, I can fight them with my light saber; I can call upon the higher powers for strength and truth.

To free myself of self-destructive thoughts, the dark side's fog must lift so I can find the love and life that have been within me and available to me all along. I fight the shadows to find the feelings and intuition that Ben Kenobi instructs Luke to trust and follow. In my struggle, I hear his words: "May the Force be with you."

nineteen

Being

To do nothing at all is the most difficult thing in the world, the most difficult and the most intellectual.

—Oscar Wilde

I am a human being not a human doing.

When I yield to the temptation of defining myself by relationships, possessions, neighborhood, profession, volunteer work, and other activities, I feel empty. My purpose is to exist; my journey is a spiritual journey of the soul. I am not a human doing; I am a human being.

So much of our lives gets caught up in pleasing others, living up to other people's expectations, and "keeping up with the Joneses." Someone once called it "living in the magazines." Psychotherapist Alice Miller terms this personality the "false self" as opposed to a personality arising from our "true self." She quotes a formerly suicidal patient in her book *The Drama of the Gifted Child:* "It seemed pointless to carry on, because in a way I had always been living a life that wasn't mine, that I didn't want, and that I was ready to throw away."[41]

I developed a false Christian personality, martyring my soul to an image of what I thought God wanted me to be. Trying to lead a life of perfection, however, consumed me. It consumed the essence of myself for years, until I was a perfect nothing. No wonder I considered suicide an option; really no big deal. Killing my body was a completion of the rest of the soul murder committed years earlier. I needed to find that human being God meant me to be.

Finding ourselves is a lifetime journey within, a lifetime of peeling off the layers of others that overlay the kernel of ourselves. When asked how she wished others to remember her, poet May Sarton said, "I guess for being fully human, if I am."[42] Our literature is richer because May Sarton wrote from her heart. What if she had spent her life trying to be another Emily Dickinson or Elizabeth Barrett Browning, instead of herself?

Some people resolve their identity crises as teenagers, while others hold to society's expectations until retirement or unemployment forces them to find their identity within themselves. After leaving the world of paid employment to stay home with my new son, my jaw would drop at the question, "What do you do?" Nurturing a little one doesn't sound nearly as exciting as trading Eurobonds. Should I have said: "Gee, it was all I could do to get my teeth brushed today; it's hard to do while holding a baby—you know, it takes two hands"? Usually I would mumble something about being at home, then quickly change the subject.

Even if pain or anxiety ties me up into one big nonfunctional knot, I don't have to feel guilty because I can't do anything. Winning medals, earning promotions, donating blood, painting the house, or getting that spaghetti stain out does not make me a valuable person. Even if I feel lifeless, some day I might wake up from this soul hibernation. Dormancy is an integral part of the natural world. Why is it so hard to bear inertia in my life when it is so much a part of the rest of the world?

God made me and all of the "original sin" they said was at my core. My job is to be the best me possible. Not the perfect pastor's daughter, not the ever-convivial corporate wife, not super mom; my job is to be me, and that is the most difficult and most important job of all.

twenty

Bad Manners

The challenge of manners is not so much to be nice to someone whose favor and/or person you covet (although more people need to be reminded of that necessity than one would suppose) as to be exposed to the bad manners of others without imitating them.

—Judith Martin[43]

Committing suicide is like dropping in on God without an invitation.

Just because I want to be someplace at a certain time doesn't mean I am welcome. Once I arrived at a friend's house for dinner twenty minutes early after losing track of the time. She faked a smile at my presence. Her husband was still in the shower. The vacuum sat on the popcorn-littered living room carpet. The baby needed a diaper change and on the counter sat dinner in the bag from the delicatessen. She had no cause for embarrassment, but I was red-faced. The invitation was for 6:00 not 5:40. I helped as much as I could, but I had not given her the opportunity to welcome me the way she had intended.

It seems to happen once each fall that I show up for church and no one is there. Sitting in the empty church, I wonder why everyone knows something I don't. I check my watch. It says 8:00 AM. Outside, the clock on the church's tower says 8:00 AM. The schedule on the front door says services are at 8:00 AM. Is it Sunday? Did God abandon me? Is this a cruel conspiracy? Did someone drop the neutron bomb? No, it is the end of daylight saving time. The time is 7:00 AM and everyone else is in bed.

What an awful feeling to be "where it isn't" when I really want to be "where it's at." Being in the wrong place at the wrong time is a common frustration dream. I have a dream where it is the end of a semester, I have forgotten about a class, and tomorrow is the final exam. Panic surges as I remember that I have yet to open the book, I have yet to attend a lecture, and there is no time to prepare. I am not where I need to be mentally or physically.

Surprise, for many people, is really shock. I even find surprise parties uncomfortable. The one surprised either feels like a stooge for not having figured out that something was up or is too polite to admit knowing all along. Everyone laughs at the expense of the guest of honor. Is this fun? Even pleasant surprises deny the one surprised the excitement of anticipation, the fun of getting ready, picking out colors, changing the menu. Unpleasant surprises are worse. To most families, suicide comes as a surprise, or more aptly, a rude shock.

Now if it is bad manners to leave our friends and families unannounced, it is even more rude to drop in on our Creator at my convenience. Here is someone "whose favor I covet" and I barge in without so much as ringing the doorbell or calling ahead. And, by the way, I'm packed to stay a long time. I wouldn't do it to a friend without some serious thought. I wouldn't do it to the mayor or president or my boss. Going someplace without an invitation or begging for an invitation risks a sharp rejection if not a less than warm reception.

That doesn't mean God isn't on call twenty-four hours a day. Good manners means I shouldn't drop in or beg; it's tacky. Anyway, it's always best to wait until the butler opens the door at fancy places.

twenty-one

Unseen Forces

The English often kill themselves. It is a malady caused by the humid climate.

—Napoleon Bonaparte

Unseen forces such as the moon's gravity or the length of sunshine in a day may be affecting my mood.

Sun spots, misaligned planets, the moon, atmospheric disturbances, stray voltage, pollution, or the seasons might be partially responsible for depression and its terminal condition, suicide. Who knows?

Think of the Bay of Fundy in eastern Canada. There, the tide's rise and fall ranges some fifty feet a day. It is the moon's gravity, and to a lesser extent the gravity of the sun, that controls the tides. Now, my thoughts leap as only a non-scientist's can. My body is 70 percent water and delicately balanced. If these unseen forces are strong enough to pull water around in the vast oceans, these pulls must have some influence over the water in me. Now, how that affects anything else, I don't know, but sometimes I do feel as if I am drowning. Or perhaps it is not the extremes of full moon and moonless nights that affect me. Perhaps it is the pushing and pulling that occurs when the going out of the tides changes to the coming in of the tides. Maybe the sloshing of my internal waters confuses me and contributes to my suicidal thoughts, making a case for waiting out this changing tide.

The moon's gravity also can affect mood and cycles of fertility. Researchers associate premenstrual syndrome with depression, anxiety, confusion, fatigue, and mood swings.[44] Seasonal Affective Disorder (SAD) is a mood disturbance produced by changes in the seasons. With this disorder, people become depressed because they don't get enough sun in the winter, while others get depressed from too much light in the summer.[45] This theory goes back over 2,000 years to Hippocrates, who wrote: "If any violent change occurred in the air according to the seasons, the brain also becomes different from what it was."

It is tragic to let confused thinking, caused by external, unseen factors, lead to confused behavior, especially when the unseen forces, when identified, are something we can wait out or treat. Recent research points to metal toxicity as a cause of Alzheimer's disease, a disease characterized by confusion. Along with aluminum, "toxins from heavy metals such as arsenic, cadmium, iron, lead, manganese, mercury, and nickel also induce in laboratory animals visible brain lesions that are similar to the neurofibrillary tangles and neuritic plaques seen in humans."[46]

Veterans of the Persian Gulf War were exposed to so many potentially toxic substances that no one knows if it is one toxin or an interaction that is causing the "Gulf War Syndrome" of symptoms. Veterans' symptoms include headaches, sleep problems, memory loss, fatigue, muscle and joint pain, respiratory and gastrointestinal problems. Toxins some veterans were exposed to include petroleum, microwaves, decontamination solutions, pesticides, pretreatment pills for nerve gas poisoning, and depleted uranium.[47, 48]

Scientists are only beginning to study the effect of environmental factors on mood and mental functioning. As more research is done some interesting information might become available for me—interesting information that might be the ray of sunshine I need.

twenty-two

Choices

When you choose anything, you reject everything else.
    —G. K. Chesterton[49]

VLADIMIR: Well? Shall we go?
ESTRAGON: Yes, let's go.
They do not move.
    —Samuel Beckett
        Waiting for Godot [50]

Other choices exist, including making no choice at all.

When it feels like the pain will consume me, it is almost impossible to look for choices. It is only possible to look for some kind of relief (and quickly, please). Other people can see choices, but then again they are not me. They are not where I am. I can see but two choices: the choice to continue in pain or do something to end it.

In *Waiting for Godot*, the two characters, Vladimir and Estragon, chose to go on ahead. Despite this choice, they stay right where they are. My life is like this existential drama. I, too, have chosen suicide and then stayed right where I was. To choose is not to act. In our do-it culture, I think I must act on every choice, but I do not have to. I can say "let's go" and then stay.

There have been times when my mind has been so frozen in pain, I did not know how much longer I could endure. When would I think clearly again? When could I see those choices obvious to everyone but me? I thought, if only I had a specific ending date, I could parcel out my meager resources to make it until then. During one of these times, I turned to astrology.

No honest therapist will forecast the ending date of a depressive episode. It isn't like measles or chicken pox, with a predictable course of exposure, incubation, illness, and recovery. I didn't expect and didn't want my therapist to tell me when it would all be over. If he did, I knew he would be lying. So I went to see someone who would give me a date.

The fortune/future-telling business is known as a haven for charlatans. Astrology, however, involves more than a card table and a crystal ball. There is a large base of knowledge associated with astrology. An astrologer needs to know how to calculate the angles of the planets, read charts, and figure out what time it was in Greenwich, England when someone was born. Although it takes a gift to be a psychic, it takes a gift and training to be an astrologer.

Still skeptical though, I called a local astrologer whom I had heard on the radio. Keeping in mind what I wanted and what I was willing to pay, I gave Leona my birthdate, birth time, and birthplace and she agreed to see me in two weeks. If this wasn't such unfamiliar territory, I would have asked if she took emergencies.

"This is the worst," she said, opening a folder with an odd chart in it. Perhaps she only needed to look at my face for that conclusion. "After today, it will start getting better." It turned out that this was a once-in-forty-years' alignment of Saturn and Uranus, or was it Pluto or Neptune? The position of Saturn was in a seven-year cycle of unusual discouragement, resistance to authority, withdrawal, and low energy. Seven years! Anyway, the planets' positions and their compounded gravity were contributing to my turbulent state of mind.

She predicted that Saturn's seven-year black cloud would hang over my head for yet another six months. Until Saturn traced its slow orbit to someplace else, I was to lie on the ground as much as possible and gather strength from Mother Earth. She also made sure I understood the need to continue seeing my therapist.

Leona gave me the ending dates to several other nasty planetary cycles, which had been combining to undo me, along with dates to buy lottery tickets. Although she said that I was lucky with investments, she didn't see me returning to the Fortune 500 financial world. It was my job in this lifetime, she explained, to learn how to relate to people, to learn how to express what is in my heart, and to write.

From the horoscope she cast, using the planets' positions at my birth, she gave me insights into the elements in my personality and past—including past lives—that were coloring my perceptions of current events. She opened up the past and future so that I could understand the impact of my present decisions. When the alternatives seemed limited and the pain seemed unending, she offered me another choice: lie on the ground and do nothing.

twenty-three

Ghosts

The misery with them all was, clearly, that they sought to interfere, for good, in human matters, and had lost the power for ever.
—Charles Dickens[51]

I might end as a ghost in limbo like Dickens' Jacob Marley, and have no recourse from my decision.

Scrooge's dead partner, Jacob Marley, in Charles Dickens' *A Christmas Carol*, roamed the earth carrying the chains he had forged and feeling the "incessant torture of remorse." Marley explains to Scrooge:

> It is required of every man, that the spirit within him should walk abroad among his fellow men, and travel far and wide; and if that spirit goes not forth in life, it is condemned to do so after death. It is doomed to wander through the world—oh, woe is me!—and witness what it cannot share, but might have shared on earth, and turned to happiness![52]

If I believe that I am without choice now, then this limbo would be totally frustrating. I am afraid of getting stuck in the middle of time and space. Edith Fiore, in *The Unquiet Dead*, writes extensively about her theories of spirit (as opposed to demonic) possession. She describes people who have died and have not gone into the "bright light." Staying on earth as spirits, they occupy other people's bodies to work out their earthly problems and create an impossible situation for possessor and possessed.

She claims to have helped many clients who suffer because spirits are interfering with the conduct of their lives. "Possessing entities who committed suicide continue to feel desolate regardless of what their hosts experience. They remain abjectly depressed."[53] Is it not me who is suicidal, but the ghost of someone who committed suicide using me? Perhaps it is some disconnected ghost that is making me feel disconnected, unreal, spacy, suicidal.

Some of these ghosts, according to Fiore, think they are still alive and feel compelled to care for a child or spouse. She describes some of these spirits as addicts who even after dying can't get enough. Many, she writes, refuse to go toward the "bright light" and their dead relatives out of shame or fear.

Now, if this isn't a double-edged sword: I may be feeling suicidal because a depressed ghost possesses me, or if I do commit suicide, I might turn into a depressed ghost. Of course, the scientific method wouldn't touch this idea with a three-hundred-page lab notebook. However unscientific this is, Fiore claims her clients experience great relief from her depossession technique.

Let's suppose her theory has some validity. The hypothesis holds that these lost souls look for people with weak vibrations from alcohol or drug abuse, illness, or stress. Ouija boards, seances, automatic writing, and channeling are also open invitations for possession by these discarnate malcontents. She cautions, "Opening up to spirits doesn't necessarily lead to possession, but if it doesn't, it's a blessing."[54] Strengthening our vibrations by surrounding ourselves with a white-light aura (like the "beam-up effect" in *Star Trek*) and abstaining from drugs and alcohol provide some protection from unwanted occupation.

If we feel possessed, Fiore suggests a "self-depossession technique" to get more control over our lives. We can try to persuade any possessing spirits to be on their way. Tell the spirits they belong in the "bright light" and that angels, guides, or the spirits of dead relatives are waiting to escort them to a peaceful, happy place.

We can assure them that no hell is worse than where they are now, and that they cannot help anyone in their present state. Like confronting a house guest whose welcome is worn out, we graciously yet firmly motivate these specters to go home. The ghost of Marley speaks, "I am here tonight to warn you, that you have yet a chance and hope of escaping my fate."[55] Ask any unwelcome visitors to leave and resolve not to become one yourself.

twenty-four

Regret

Why should the dead be wiser than the living? The dead know only this—that it was better to be alive.

—James Elroy Flecker[56]

Those with near-death experiences after suicide attempts report regret for what they did and a renewed commitment to life.

The near-death experiences of people revived after heart attacks and car accidents have captured my imagination. Survivors relate all-encompassing feelings of bliss and love and peace, and it sounds wonderful. It sounds like everything I dream of, until I hear about the near-death experiences of those who try to commit suicide. Although some experience the love—with a message—others experience worse.

Writing about suicide survivors, near-death researcher P. M. H. Atwater states: "The experience is not magic. Surviving does not make you enlightened or superhuman....The vast majority of near-death survivors have come to realize that hurrying your death is no escape and guarantees nothing."[57]

One suicide survivor said that he had not thought of suicide since his near-death experience and that suicide was "a copout to me and not the way to heaven...it is a terrible waste." Survivors use their near-death experience as a resource to help them work out their problems. The feeling they bring back from "over there" is that the real work can only be done "back here." Research finds that some of these near-death experiencers are "notably renewed and refreshed by that feeling, using their near-death event as a source of courage, strength, and inspiration."[58]

Angie Fenimore writes in *Beyond the Darkness: My Near-Death Journey to the Edge of Hell and Back* of her experience immediately following an overdose of pills. Her brief journey into the darkness changed her life, left her grateful for another chance to live, and compelled her to share her story with others who are suicidal. If we don't resolve our problems here, she cautions, "we take our earthly baggage with us."[59] After reading her chilling account of Hell's threshold, I still struggle with suicidal thoughts, but my fantasy of a blissful "other side" is gone.

A near-death experience resulting from a suicide attempt is not always hellish, nor is it always a deterrent. One woman tried suicide twice after her peaceful near-death experience, but ultimately realized "there was no escape." She knew she had "better get busy and solve her problems."[60] Another woman mentioned being trapped with her problem on the other side. "It was still around, even when I was 'dead.' And it was like it was repeating itself."[61]

I have not had a near-death experience; however, I have had a pre-life experience. At one point, a hypnotherapist age-regressed me back to the womb. I felt terrified that my mother was trying to kill me. Trying to ease this primal agitation, he asked me to go back to where I was before I entered the womb. Still deeply relaxed, I went back to a place of pure light and tranquility. For the first time in my life, I was aware of what peace and love felt like. He helped me remember this light, not experience it for the first time. Now, when I need comfort, I can remember it again.

twenty-five

Reincarnation

There is no past, and there is no future. There is only now, and you can't get out of it.

—Alan Watts[62]

If there is reincarnation, I might have to come back and suffer this again.

The Hindus say I could come back as a mouse. That may not be nearly as bad as coming back as a human being. Returning to earth and starting over at life, from the beginning, is an overwhelming thought. Why would I want to come back and go through my childhood again, go through my teenage years again, go through this downhill spiral again? Do I really want to turn this horror show into a double matinee?

If I keep working on this project, difficult as it is, some day I might finish. I took trigonometry three times in college. Twice, I dropped the class because I thought a different teaching assistant or different time of day would make it easier. Alas, the third time I started trigonometry, I knew I couldn't drop it without delaying my graduation. I would have to bear with the early morning hour, the boring lecturer, and my all-too-apparent lack of ability in the subject. Taking my lowest grade ever, I passed; I could go on.

Psychologists have a theory called the "compulsion to repetition."[63] According to this theory, we subconsciously create situations parallel to our unresolved experiences attempting to resolve them. In the same way that dreams are a way to resolve the day's events, the mind creates events to resolve our past like marrying someone with traits just like mom or dad or an ex-spouse or taking a job in a company that feels just like "family."

Taking this idea of repetition further, perhaps this life is a working out of the unsettled events of past lives. Maybe in a former life I was the abuser, and in this life, I need to learn what it is like to be the victim. I wouldn't want to repeat that lesson from the start. Maybe in a former life I committed suicide, and this time around I have to learn to appreciate the life I have. For me, that is a tough lesson, and sometimes, I think I have dropped that class in a few lifetimes. This time, I know I must complete this prerequisite to go on to other classes; I'll take the low grade instead of the incomplete.

Receiving the consequences of past life actions in this life is a foundation of the Buddhist and Hindu ideas of karma. *Karma* is the Sanskrit word for "action." With karma, present actions determine future events in this lifetime and our destiny in the next. Charles Breaux writes in *The Way of Karma* that karma is "our most diligent teacher. The dynamics of karma are not only the basis for defining our individual characters, but the healing and development of the psyche, in truth the soul."[64]

I don't know what I did in a former lifetime to get here, but if I give up now, I create more messes to work out in the next life. Stop. It's bad enough this time, maybe I should learn my lessons, and create some good karma to enjoy next time around. I'd like to do myself a future favor and survive. Already, I have gone through enough pain piling up the experience and insights I have up to this point; I don't want that struggle to go to waste.

Different lessons are waiting for each of us. Facing terminal illness, some people commit suicide. Faced with deteriorating mental capacity or attractiveness, some people commit suicide. Faced with the breakup of a relationship, the death of a spouse, or a prison sentence, some people commit suicide. Aren't there lessons in playing out those difficult hands? Aren't there opportunities for spiritual growth, if not the accumulation of good karma in those adverse circumstances?

The toughest lesson for me was not trigonometry, but learning how to reach out and receive the help and kindness of others. I needed to learn that people can be caring, respectful, and trustworthy. For me, learning the lessons of life may equal one of the twelve labors of Hercules. (I'm thinking of the one where he had to clean out the thirty years' dirt in the stables of King Augeus' three thousand oxen.) I can't harness rivers for my project, but, with help, I can clean out the manure of this and other lifetimes so I don't have to come back and start the work all over.

twenty-six

Role Model

I think maybe I am a good role model from the point of view of simply persisting and having the psychic energy and the—whatever it is—to go on.

—May Sarton[65]

Whether I like it or not, I am a role model, discouraging and encouraging others by my behavior.

Call it the domino theory or whatever, suicides can occur in clusters and run in families. There are many examples of communities where teens have killed themselves in rapid succession. There are all too many examples of families with a history of suicides.

Starting in February 1983, eight suicides and at least sixteen attempts in the next fourteen months occurred in Plano, Texas. In 1984, the tri-county area north of New York City saw eight suicides in four months. Although the teens did not know each other, the failure of one individual to hang on was enough to trigger others to let go. We are all mountain climbers strung together on the rope of life; we rely on others to hold on so we don't fall.

Researchers have concluded that clustered suicides are not infrequent. One person's suicide may "lower the threshold for vulnerable people in the same geographic vicinity." After the cluster of New York suicides, Westchester psychiatrist Samuel Klagsbrun said, "When one kid actually goes ahead and does the unthinkable, it's almost as if it gives permission to others to also do the unthinkable."[66]

Another's negativism can bring us down, but human energy can also lift us up. When someone moves into a neighborhood and cleans up the dumpiest house on the block, others notice and respond. The fixing up and picking up gets others motivated to take a little more pride in their own house. It raises the neighborhood's standards. It may even raise property values.

We live in community and our energy goes out from us and energy from others comes back to us, no matter how isolated we might feel. An infrared picture shows our heat. Some psychics read people's auras, seeing, with their gifted vision, the colors of the energy surrounding the body as a key to health. Even if I can't live for myself, by resisting suicide, I set a quiet example. I project a positive aura.

Giving in to suicidal thoughts somehow sanctions this behavior. How would the boys in my Cub Scout den react if their leader let go of her grip on life? If they ever get lost in an emotional woods, I want them to remember that their leader didn't give up, but pointed out a star to guide them. What kind of message does society send our young people when we endorse assisted suicide for those with crushing pain? Young people experience crushing pain too. No one wants to show children that it's all right to play with matches, fly kites in power lines, cross the street without looking, or give up in the face of adversity. No one wants to tell others by their behavior that suicide is OK.

twenty-seven

My Children

Sometimes I feel like a motherless child, a long way from home.
—Sorrow Song[67]

Day care for my children is more expensive than therapy for me.

It's hard to justify spending money for therapy, but if I look at the cost of day care, therapy looks like a bargain. The cost of quality day care has made me pause long enough to consider my children's longer term emotional needs as well. For a child, the death of a parent is emotionally devastating, but the impact of a death by suicide is especially profound.

Children perceive the death of a parent as personal rejection and abandonment. Many children think it was their fault. The impact is difficult to put in the past tense as the child struggles with the daily reminders of the absent parent: one less around the table, the loss of income, fewer hugs, and mismatched socks. For an adult, the death of a parent is still considered one of the most traumatic events of life.

Once, while in college, I had started to worry after not seeing my friend for a week. Then I ran into her and her fiance sitting on a bench in the school's basement corridor. Her body was tight to the wall, as if drawing strength from the concrete. Her ashen skin and pale blond hair blended into the cement like an ancient Roman bas-relief. When she saw me, her red eyes rose from an ocean of greyness; I sputtered hello. Bill answered my silent questions, "We just got back from her mother's funeral; overdose of sleeping pills, not her first."

"Oh, I'm so sorry," I mumbled. My heart should have opened to her, but I had built up so many walls around my own pain, I only felt sick and left quickly. With so much unrealized business of my own, I couldn't care for her the way a friend should. In my tightly ordered world, there was no room for problems: mine or those of anyone else. There was little room for emotion either in the sealed vacuum of my psyche; there couldn't be if my world was to hold together. Nauseated, I ran to my apartment and called my mother, looking for reassurance that my world was perfect.

This suicide set me back. In little ways, I had started to see my parents for what they were. Living away from their shadow for the first time, I had begun separating my ideal from their reality. This shock sent me back to romanticizing and pretending. There I was, back to my myths: parents are saints; honor your father and mother; they did the best they could. I put my feelings in repression's deep freezer and thought more about pulling the plug than chipping away the frost.

Unlike my friend's mother, my mother is living, available for study in the present tense. Every time I interact with her, I pick up clues to verify my perceptions and insights. Her current behavior reinforces the choices I made as an adult. They also explain the choices I made as a child. My friend can't do that. It's almost impossible to look upon the dead realistically. It is hard to see the dead as having been human beings with human characteristics, frailties, and mental illnesses that continue to influence the living. In our society, we "don't speak ill of the dead." It is difficult for my friend to understand her childhood when she can't see her mother in the present with the eyes of an adult.

My friend has siblings, but this event has clouded their perceptions too. They want to remember their mother nobly struggling with her mental illness. What was it like to be a child in this woman's home? Was her behavior confusing, erratic, abusive? As children, did they hold themselves responsible? Wasn't it lonely? Beyond loneliness, however, is the danger of having no outlet for the complex feelings created by the suicide of a parent.

A National Academy of Sciences report on grief states, "For children, the suicide of a parent or sibling not only presents immediate difficulties, but is thought by many observers to result in lifelong vulnerability to mental health problems."[68] Unresolved grief and guilt can even lead to a fatal identification with the dead. The parent has powerfully modeled what they considered permissible behavior.

So I stay alive. Although I am not the engaged, responsive mother I want to be, I will be alive to pay what I need to for my mistakes and to allow my children's anger to have a living target. My children shouldn't have to idealize me or assume the liability for my actions. I must take responsibility for my behavior and for my children's welfare. Today, this week, day care is more expensive than therapy. Over the course of a lifetime, day care is a short-term expense, while therapy is a long-term investment. For their sakes, I make the investment, and, in time, there will be dividends to split.

twenty-eight

Friends

I have learned that the subtle art of rejection used with finesse, can be every bit as abusive as a punch in the face.

—Gordon Parks[69]

Suicide disturbs even casual acquaintances of the past and present.

Who might be saddened, or at least caused to gasp, if I did myself in? Mercy at the bank, Ruth at the grocery store, Norman next door, all might feel hurt. Mrs. S., my old Girl Scout leader, Ms. B., my high school counselor, Peg, my college roommate, Dennis, Joanne, and Glenn, my former co-workers, all might feel a bit betrayed. What would my tenth grade English teacher think? These people knew me in better times. They remember the better times even if I can't.

The grief of close relatives is clear when anybody dies; however, the grief of those on the periphery of a person's life can also be profound. Mary McGlothin Davis writes in the *Personnel Journal*, "co-worker suicides are painful."[70] She describes the group therapy efforts mounted at her place of employment when a co-worker committed suicide. Along with shock and grief, employees feel anger toward the deceased, other co-workers and health care workers, as well. They feel cheated out of an opportunity to talk their co-worker out of it. Those who worked closely with the individual feel responsible. Schools go through similar grieving when a student dies.

In an article titled "Living with Chronic Illness," Stephen Schmidt writes: "We do not live alone.... When one dies, others die too, not completely, but a little. So the person deciding to end life ends a whole series of relationships, relationships that depend on that person."[71]

Many communities are trying to reach out to those members who are considering suicide. Some communities have set up hot lines and task forces, but remained vexed about how to reach those closed off in fear, hurt, loneliness, confusion, and shame. Throughout the nation, various groups have made suicide prevention phone services available.

The local operator at 1-555-1212 or the toll-free operator at 1-800-555-1212 has current information on hot line phone numbers. There are people who want to listen at the other end of the phone right now. I used to squirm when articles suggested calling others. The phone was too intimidating, too intimate; the people on the other end probably couldn't understand if I tried to explain or would respond inappropriately.

If I could have trusted others more, I might not have backed myself into this corner. Somebody would have steered me toward help much sooner. I don't ever have to trust anyone completely, but deciding to trust, just a little, made reaching out possible.

Starting hot lines and task forces are important, but somehow it needs to enter the consciousness of everyone that life is not cheap. We can all protect and nurture each other by little actions every day. As a society and as individuals, we need to practice human decency at every turn.

Kindness can stop the angry gestures and big hurts from decaying lives into hopelessness. Like the biblical symbols of salt and yeast, the smallest positive gestures can make a big difference. Friends, even remote acquaintances, are important to consider.

twenty-nine

My Husband

A man's dying is more the survivor's affair than his own.
—Thomas Mann[72]

My husband could never find everything he needs to file the income taxes.

My husband would have no one to balance the checkbook, collect the stuff to do the income taxes, and pay the bills, and he couldn't do it himself. (He would do like my elderly neighbor: dump the mail on the table; when the pile is too high, put it in a box; when the box is too full, throw it all out.) In all fairness, I married him because he loves to scrub floors, do dishes, and mow the grass, not because I could make him into an accountant.

Household finances are my department and I purposely keep him in the dark and purposely keep the files disorganized. It's a survival game. I tell myself: "You can't leave until after you clean out that filing cabinet and organize the receipts in those shoe boxes so he can find everything." Where there is a mess, there is a reason to live.

Love and fear for my husband have also led me to keep him in the dark about the depth of my suicidal feelings. I didn't want to upset him unnecessarily. The thoughts would go away tomorrow, anyway, wouldn't they? I was afraid he would go away if I told him how I really felt. Why would I jeopardize our relationship?

Several times, I did tell him how I felt, and he dismissed the feelings as transient. Through his own fear and denial, he didn't follow up to find out if my thoughts persisted. Through my own fear and denial, I didn't want further discussion.

At some point, I picked up a book about relationship addiction. There I was on the first page. In fact, the author implied that 96 percent of the population suffered from this addiction. Yes, I was a relationship addict; addicted to the few I had. Yes, I used my husband; I borrowed his will to live. Now, if I saw myself as a relationship addict, I could feel guilty about that, too.

Yet, I worried that if I cured myself of this addiction, I might not have enough of my own will to live, and then what? If this is a disease, I don't want the cure. Most of the time, the main reason I stay alive is for my husband and children. Is it a disease to be dependent on people for their juice of aliveness when my own juice has run out?

When someone is dependent on me, that should be reason enough to stay alive. Perhaps fostering this dependence is a mentally healthy thing to do. I don't think it's wrong to keep the income tax files in such disarray that only I can find anything. Moreover, I worry about how close I am to the edge whenever I straighten up a closet. I'll admit it's not healthy, but it is life-affirming behavior in its own eccentric way.

My mind garbles the concepts of dependence, independence, and responsibility. I do know, however, about interdependence: about me paying the bills and him scrubbing the floor; and there is something right about that. There is something right about staying alive out of a sense of duty. Duty may not arise from love, and sometimes it is sick, but it does make me stop. It makes me stop long enough to seek out the love within myself and the world around me. When I find this love, when I can finally feel my husband's love, duty no longer will be an issue.

thirty

Love

That Love is all there is,
Is all we know of Love.
—Emily Dickinson[73]

━━━

Suicide denies me the opportunity to find out how much love is in the world and in myself.

What is love? Except for valentine sentiment and movie sexuality, I didn't know what love was. It was an abstract idea to me. In Sunday School, I was commanded to "love my neighbor as myself." Love was something I should *do* like brushing my teeth or making my bed, not something I could feel. I tried to act loving—remembering birthdays, giving baby showers, entertaining friends—but love isn't an act, it's a feeling, and I couldn't feel.

Until I had the experience of being age-regressed back to before I was in the womb, I hadn't felt love. In that hypnotic, pre-womb state, I felt the love from which I came and understood my deepest purpose was to find love and give love. It wasn't a new feeling; it was an old feeling newly remembered. Through the years, I had encased the feeling of love in a lead-lined box deep within my heart. In not wanting the love destroyed, I had cut myself off from all feelings and had virtually forgotten how to feel at all. Shielding my psyche by not allowing myself to feel—the bad or the good—began as an act of self-preservation, but now it was leading to my destruction.

Once, I read of a woman in Israel who heard terrorists coming up the beach toward her house. Living close to the border and prepared for such an emergency, she grabbed the most precious thing in her life, her baby, and headed for her hiding place. She held the baby close to keep it from crying out.

As the terrorists entered her house and neared her hiding place, she held the baby tighter. Soon the intruders left. Relieved, she emerged from the cramped closet. To her horror, when she unwrapped her baby, he was dead. She had accidentally smothered him.

The love I am so desperately trying to hold onto suffocates as I try to save it. In the face of enormous pain, trauma, and guilt, I irrevocably smother my original source of love by my suicidal thoughts. I wrap up my most precious resource of love so tightly, so others can't destroy it, that I also lose access to it.

This is the paradox of repression. Although repression allowed me to survive by not exposing me to the full frontal assault of my traumatic experiences, it also blocked any feelings of love and happiness. Freud wrote that repression pushes back conscious feelings into the unconscious mind.[74] This pushing uses energy and is the source of much pain and fatigue.

In deciding not to commit suicide, I also decide to peel back the layers of repression to find the lost treasure of love inside myself. After I have found the love in myself, then I can feel all the love in the world. How much love is in the world for me? I won't find out if I don't stay to look.

thirty-one

Success

Force is all-conquering, but its victories are short-lived.
   —Abraham Lincoln

What if I succeed when I only mean to cry for help?

What if I succeed and really mean to fail? Some suicide
attempts are desperate demonstrations of seriousness,
penance, or frustration. More than escaping and disconnecting from others, some suicide attempts are attempts to
connect. Trying to wake up or change other people through
suicidal gestures, however, is a dangerous game. There are
many cases of people taking carefully timed drug overdoses,
half-expecting someone to find them before the full effect
of the poison sets in. When that person doesn't come in
time because of a flat tire, a phone call, or traffic, a gesture
turns into self-murder.

   Often I have heard myself say: "I'll show them. When
I'm gone, then they'll be sorry. Now my parents (or therapist or insurance company or whatever) will understand I
am serious." My feelings are so mixed up, I can't begin to
tell them how I feel. Like bow-lines and half-hitches, knots
are easier to show than verbalize. Showing them how serious
I am seems more understandable than explaining. Yet,
somehow I need to try the verbal approach again because
the demonstration is far too dangerous.

It is hard to tell my therapist that the reason I am calling at 10 PM is because I cannot hold the receiver and the glass of water and the pills simultaneously. Do I say, "Look, as long as I am on the phone, at least one hand and my mouth are busy"? Maybe he can't understand how serious I am because I am ashamed of expressing my suicidal feelings. Why do I consider suicidal thoughts more shameful than suicidal actions? It takes conscious, continuous effort to overcome being ashamed of my feelings.

How can I tell my insurance company that I live for my weekly visits? They simply can't cut me back to twice a month. They don't know how I feel, however, unless I tell them explicitly. Once, I told an insurance company nurse that if money was the problem, I would help them lower their costs by reducing their "covered lives" by one. She let me keep my once a week visits and called me later in the day to find out if I was OK. From that encounter, I learned that I could get my needs met if I spoke clearly about how I felt. As for my parents, I don't think they could ever take me seriously. I could make them feel guilty, but hurting myself can't make them love me.

Attempting suicide as a means of communication makes a dangerous point, but is it the point I really want to make? There is also the possibility that I'll have to pay full price to make that point, and is that worth it? If I live through the experience, I will have violated the trust of others and hurt those I didn't intend to hurt along with those I had every intention of waking up. If I am acting out of guilt, this can only create more guilt, not absolve or justify my actions or feelings.

Attempting suicide creates changes, but not necessarily the changes I want. Do I want to give a judge and my family the right to control my treatment? Do I want others to fear leaving me alone or fear being with me? Do I want people to distrust and doubt me? The words come with difficulty, but I must try words again and not actions.

thirty-two

Failure

I am the only guinea pig I have.
—R. Buckminster Fuller

—————

What if I fail and severely disable myself when I truly wanted to die?

Describing suicide with the loaded words *success, attempt,* and *failure,* is a reflection of society's ambiguous relationship with the life force. We use similar words regarding abortion. People speak of "failed suicide attempts," and I cringe. In a battle where the life force won over great odds, failure is not the result. For a struggle that resulted in a second chance in this world, the word *failure* doesn't fit.

Sometimes the life force winning results in no permanent scars; more often the warfare leaves lifelong wounds. I doubt that anyone would deliberately inflict the torture of a backfired suicide attempt on themselves. In agony, people seek escape from their pain through suicide. In return, they have traded it for a different agony. How I wish I didn't have to learn from them, but I think they would like it if I did.

The son of a woman my husband worked with years ago despaired of life. The teen doused himself with gasoline and set himself on fire in the backyard. Miraculously, he did not die. However, he spent many excruciating months in intensive care. The hospital bill was over a million dollars. Others understood the value of his life and saved him. Now, he also understands the value of his life. I have felt the pain that made him want to escape the world. Knowing his story, though, I fear creating even more pain for myself in suicide.

After failed drug overdoses, some suffer liver and neurological damage. Brain damage can result from a failed hanging attempt. Some who have tried electrocution have had to have their arms amputated. Jumpers have suffered multiple broken bones and paralysis when their attempts have gone awry. Guns misfire or kick back unpredictably. The details are gruesome. These people were and are in serious pain. They have found reasons to live despite compromised health.

"Assisted suicides" also have horror stories about the life force's struggle to prevail over death. Ann Wickett Humphry, former wife of Hemlock Society president Derek Humphry, made a videotape shortly before her death. She said in the video that in assisting the double suicide of her parents with Derek, her mother had started to choke on the pills. Instead of helping her vomit, she held a bag over her mother's mouth. She confessed, "I walked away from that house thinking we're both murderers."[75]

She alleged that Derek told her that he smothered his first wife, Jean, after she had begun to vomit an overdose of drugs. He denied the charge and asked, "Where's the evidence?"[76] Indeed, the only witness is dead. Was this death a peaceful "assisted suicide" or murder?

The words of the right-to-die movement sound compassionate, logical, dignified, and honest. This country was founded in the spirit of assuring individual freedoms and rights. We love that word *right*; it sounds so right. Our forebears, however, expressed in the Constitution our right to "*life*, liberty, and the pursuit of happiness." In reality, the right-to-die movement is a mocking of our other rights, appealing directly to laziness and despair. This planet would have failed long ago if life were not stronger than hopelessness. Perhaps I can let the life force win without testing it. I would rather not find out how strong it really is.

thirty-three

Law

Why murder is the greatest of all crimes is not that the life taken may be that of an Abraham Lincoln, but because it might be yours or mine.

—F. Tennyson Jesse

A suicide is subject to criminal investigation and for good reason.

The police treat every suicide as foul play, questioning witnesses and family members, searching the effects for evidence, turning the body over to the coroner for autopsy. The law binds the coroner or medical examiner to investigate every suicide to reach the exact cause and time of death and to rule out homicide. Investigators may read diaries, school essays, and letters to be sure of the deceased's intentions and to be sure someone else didn't have a gun to their head when the suicide note was written. Those closest are suspects; they may be subpoenaed and have to give depositions. Besides the police, life insurance companies may have their own investigation so they can get out of paying a survivor's claim through a suicide loophole.

A person I knew was found hung from the rafters of his mother's attic. On the surface it was a suicide, but an investigation by the police and an autopsy revealed what happened. He had died of auto-erotic asphyxiation, an often fatal form of masturbation where a person deliberately cuts off oxygen to the brain to enhance arousal. The investigation was embarrassing but necessary to rule the death an accident. The law needs to distinguish accidents from suicides.

In August of 1991, the body of freelance writer Joseph Daniel Casolaro was found in a West Virginia motel. At the time of his death, Casolaro was investigating the theft of highly sophisticated software from a small firm named Inslaw. Trying to link the theft to the U.S. and world intelligence communities, Casolaro had been working on a book he called *The Octopus*.

After delaying family notification for several days, the medical examiner ruled that the physical evidence held "nothing inconsistent with suicide." [77] His family and colleagues roundly questioned the ruling and the delay. There are many complex issues surrounding the theft, his research, and his death. If he had willingly committed suicide, he left an important project in disarray. However, he knew enough crucial evidence to make murder a possibility. A fellow journalist observes: "The cause of Casolaro's death may be forever relegated to that area of uncertainty reserved for so many conspiracy theories."[78]

Investigators are still working on the 1993 death of Vincent Foster, a senior attorney in the Clinton administration. Did he have information other people did not want him to reveal? Was he a part of a larger conspiracy? Was he simply fed up with the world? Many wish he were alive to answer one more question: was it suicide or murder?

Suicide is far too close to murder to dismiss without legal scrutiny. Real and fictional super sleuths have been working on the classic mystery plot of suicide versus homicide for centuries. Driving someone to commit suicide or forcing someone into it could be the perfect crime, for one doesn't have to dispose of the body. Physical coercion, however, is not always obvious, and psychological terrorism can be as effective.

Legalizing suicide may subtly coerce those with illnesses who need others to care for them. The ill may want to live but feel they are a burden to their families or society and may commit suicide to spare those close to them. If assisted suicide becomes legitimate, people may feel obligated to die when they really want to live or feel ambiguous about ending their life. Legalizing suicide sends the message that society doesn't want imperfect people, or is too lazy or greedy to care for them. Pain provokes enough suicides; the law should not provoke more.

Common sense suggests that suicide remain subject to investigation, primarily because the only witness is dead. In too many cases, there is little difference between suicide and murder or suicide and an accident. The legal system needs to be primarily responsible for weighing that difference and factoring in possible coercion. Legalizing suicide and assisted suicide is dangerously close to legalizing and legitimizing murder: my murder.

thirty-four

Shame on Me

Judgment comes from experience—and experience comes from bad judgment.
—Brig. Gen. J. W. Lang[79]

Even a court should not decide if I deserve capital punishment for my behavior.

I may burn with guilt, but society judges that only the worst crimes warrant the death penalty. Still, many of our states don't have the death penalty and many people don't believe in capital punishment no matter what crime is committed.

The members of Amnesty International are fighting to end capital punishment around the world. They write, "Like torture, the death penalty is cruel, inhuman and degrading. It destroys human lives and violates human rights." [80] They argue that it does not fulfill societal needs in a way no other punishment can.

For me to pronounce this sentence on myself is unjust and high-handed. No matter how ashamed I am of my behavior, I shouldn't sentence myself to death. Yet the language of guilt reinforces how I feel when I make a mistake: "I was so embarrassed, I wanted to die," or "It killed me to see her cry," or "Oh, shoot." Suicide is the ultimate self-punishment, but it can also be a way of avoiding facing responsibility for my actions.

When inmates commit suicide in jail, they may take their lives out of guilt, but does it help their victims? Teenagers who commit suicide after wrecking the family car create even more heartache for their families. Faced with financial reverses, how can suicide solve a family's credit problems? History books report that when the stock market lost $30 billion in October 1929 bankers and financiers jumped out of windows. Do these acts expiate guilt or do they leave a bigger mess for others? Under intense stress, suicide looks like the only way out of a problem; but in the cold light of day, it looks like the easy way.

The cumulative shame of a whole life does not add up to death. It may take years to acknowledge the full results of my behavior, but I need to take responsibility for my actions. Facing responsibilities may demand extraordinary courage, the level of which no one else may ever recognize. Using death as an excuse or an escape is a mistake I cannot learn from. It takes time to clear away the confusion. It takes time to work on a positive way to express regret. Yet I need time to show that I have grown through my bad judgment calls, poor choices, and impulsive decisions and that I am worthy of a second chance.

Moreover, some of my shame may rightly belong to others, and I need time to sort that out, too, before taking responsibility for everything.

thirty-five

Shame on Them

When two elephants fight, it is the grass that suffers.
—Kikuyu Proverb

Someone else's abusive behavior shouldn't mean a death sentence for me.

I do not have to take responsibility for my parents, grandparents, other relatives, baby-sitters, or neighbors abusing me as a child or teenager. I am not responsible for the messes made by their alcoholism or their low self-esteem. They may have been abused or neglected, but this does not excuse their failure to grow up and act responsibly. Having suffered enough at their hands, I do not deserve to suffer further at my own hand.

It is a trial worthy of a saint's suffering to live in a home or work on a job with people who abuse me. In the third century, Saint Barbara's father forced her to spend her youth in a locked tower, then lopped off her head after a tutor converted her to Christianity. Even if life isn't that bad, it is agonizing to feel that no one is listening. When those closest to me give the family dog more respect and affection than they do me, life seems too long. But I should not continue their torture and kill myself. They still wouldn't understand how I feel; they still wouldn't appreciate me.

As a teenager, I had one dream: to move out of the house as soon as I could. Putting all of my energy toward this dream, I earned good grades and won scholarships. The money I earned babysitting, cleaning, and working in a dime store went into the bank, not into records, clothes, and movies like my friends. Finally, I left at seventeen. With scholarships, loans, and part-time jobs, I supported myself through college, graduated, and started to work. I had reached my goal, but it was the only goal I had. Having reached it, I felt profoundly empty. Concerned only with survival, I had no other dreams, no sense of self, and no purpose. I became depressed, or perhaps only now could I begin to feel the depression that was there all along. Like someone with post-traumatic stress syndrome, I did what I had to do to survive, then collapsed.

The damage inflicted by sexual, emotional, and physical abuse may appear superficial at the time, but it is deep. Suicide is an extension of this abuse. Even if my parents are incapable of showing love and respect, this does not mean that I don't deserve it, that I don't deserve to live. Should I die on the gamble they might regret their abuse or that my death would punish them with guilt? There is a possibility it would grieve them; however, suicide may turn them into the *victims*. They would love to be the innocent victims and receive other people's pity and sympathy for what was done to them; it allows them to forget what they did to me.

Now, who receives the punishment? Those who deny themselves life suffer the greater punishment. Those who deny themselves the chance to heal, to question the abuser's effects, to see justice served, suffer the most, by far. For victims, staying alive can be an act of revenge. A strong, clear victim will make any criminal afraid. As the pirate Israel Hands said in *Treasure Island,* "Dead men don't bite."[81]

thirty-six

Stories

The ancient people perceived the world and themselves within that world as part of an ancient continuous story composed of innumerable bundles of other stories.

—Leslie Marmon Silko[82]

Society, by definition, includes the stories of everyone, even the most despicable person: me.

Talk-show producers and hosts know something I often forget: my story is important, not only for myself but for others too. In an interdependent community, we are not simply Peeping Toms when fascinated by sensational murders or lifestyle oddities. Our fascination arises because they mirror a small piece of ourselves. The tabloids wouldn't sell if we couldn't relate in some symbolic way to the alien encounters or the woman with a monster head. Although my story isn't nearly so odd or interesting, it is at least as important because it also reflects a part of the society I live in.

The success of many support groups and Twelve Step-type programs rests in the sharing of stories. Individual talk-therapy also relies heavily on a sharing of stories. It takes brass to get our stories out even in an anonymous television studio. There is a need to hear them; there is a need to share them. Whether it is the act of getting it off our chests, the chemistry of the group, or the content or context, millions have found healing in the oral sharing of their stories.

Others use journals, diaries, music, art, and dance to express themselves, communicate, connect with the rest of society, and heal. I always thought I was a horrible artist: blob-topped trees, stick people without an inch of space for a heart and the boniest of arms and hands, rainbows of awning stripes, and yellow-ball suns with eight symmetrical rays. At the suggestion of a book,[83] I picked up some large, chunky toddler crayons and drawing paper at the art supply store. Using my non-dominant hand, I began to scribble, then draw and write. It was fun. Did I say *fun?* That isn't a word I use to describe many of the therapies I have tried, but this was different for me, and I found that my left hand was quite artistic and had some interesting things to say. My left hand told me stories about myself I still can't believe, but some day I will.

Artists, musicians, and writers throughout the ages have used their work as catharsis, creating pieces that speak directly to our hearts. The disciplines of art therapy, music therapy, and dance therapy use creative expression to promote healing by helping us connect to our own and others' feelings. Besides their theories, it makes me feel better to turn up the radio at a favorite song and key into a lyric that captures my emotions exactly. That makes for double tragedy when someone like singer/songwriter Kurt Cobain commits suicide. He no longer can help us connect with the universality of our emotions because his suicide is a permanent disconnect. He has become some otherworldly icon.

Even the suicide of someone as despicable as Adolf Hitler disconnects his story from ours, makes him into a figure of mythology rather than a product of our society. In the book, *For Your Own Good: Hidden Cruelty in Child-Rearing and the Roots of Violence,* psychotherapist Alice Miller reconstructs Hitler's personal history. She offers chilling insights into Hitler's early environment, his brutal, lonely childhood, and the effects of unrelenting abuse on the development of his conscience. Miller writes that we live in danger of another Hitler unless the "public becomes aware that countless children are subjected to soul murder every day and that society as a whole must suffer as a result."[84] Can we hear the story of Hitler's life, however, over the noise and distance of his death? Has he become so much the personification of Satan that we cannot see our story in his?

What about that even more despicable character: me? Difficult as it is to put together any pieces of my story in such a fractured state of mind, others need my story too. What about the support group I haven't joined? Those people might need my story. What about members of my family? They may not want to hear it, but they need this story too. I judge myself so harshly I can't imagine any importance to my history, my present, or my future. Yet my story is an important part of a much larger, much longer, and much better story because my chapter is in it. Is that hard to imagine? Just ask Oprah or Phil.

thirty-seven

Marilyn Monroe

It's possible I am pushing through solid rock
in flintlike layers, as the ore lies, alone;
I am such a long way in I see no way through,
and no space: everything is close to my face,
and everything close to my face is stone.

—Rainer Maria Rilke
    Translated by Robert Bly[85]

Marilyn Monroe was glamorous; her suicide was not.

Marilyn Monroe read the works of Joyce, Proust, Shelley, Whitman, Keats, and Rilke. She admired Lincoln and Einstein. While still known as Norma Jeane Baker, she told a photographer she wanted to go to Columbia University to study law. Those who knew her described her as bright. There was more to her than the allure of her vulnerability. There was more to her than her death.

The legendary death of Marilyn Monroe has probably done more to glamorize suicide than any other death in the last half-century. Her suicide has been an unfortunate inspiration to some and a morbid fascination for many. Focusing on her death and stereotypical media image, we fail to recognize her humanity.

Norma Jeane Baker spent her childhood in a series of foster homes with several years in an orphanage between homes. Her mother was living, although institutionalized with a depressive disorder. Her father was never more than a photograph and a fantasy. As if the repeated abandonments weren't enough emotional abuse, she was also sexually and physically abused in some of the foster homes.

In her book *Marilyn*, Gloria Steinem writes that Marilyn recalled a sexual attack at age eight by a man who paid her a nickel. After telling her foster mother of the incident, the woman slapped her and asked her how she dared say such things. Marilyn recalled later, "I was so hurt, I began to stammer. She didn't believe me! I cried that night in bed all night; I just wanted to die."[86]

A year later, her guardian brought her to the orphanage. "When a young girl feels lost and lonely and that nobody wants her," she said, "it's something she never can forget as long as she lives."[87] One can imagine her spending her lifetime trying to heal the abandonment, looking for someone to love her as no one did as a child.

In an era when Oedipal theories equated trauma with delusion, difficult childhood experiences were discounted. Tranquilizers numbed the pain of being misunderstood both as a child and as an adult. In her struggle, she tried desperately to escape her pain and understand her fears and compulsions. To the end, she sought the resolution of her traumas through friendship, medication, and psychotherapy.

Marilyn Monroe's professional success, despite the lack of nurturing and the abuse, shows character not often associated with her image. In looking at the life she tried to live, in taking her experiences seriously, we recognize her strength and determination as well as her vulnerability. We can copy her fortitude. However, it is no honor to her memory to copy an act of desperation. Marilyn Monroe was glamorous. Her suicide was not; it was tragic.

thirty-eight

Heroism

What a hero one can be without moving a finger.
—Henry David Thoreau[88]

Suicide denies me the chance to be my own hero, my own rescuer.

Throw yourself a life preserver. Dive in after yourself and swim yourself to shore. You would do it for a stranger. Now, do it for yourself. Extend a pole. Throw a lifeline. Pull yourself into the boat and row yourself to shore. Now, give yourself a medal because you have achieved the most formidable feat on the planet: you have saved yourself. There may be no witness to recognize it, but congratulations! You and I know, and the rest can only guess, anyway.

Give yourself a hug. Look in the mirror and say, "Job well done; you have made it another day." No one else can imagine how hard it was to make it through today, but you and I can appreciate that you are a hero for saving your life.

Webster's defines *heroism* as "brave, noble actions or traits" and a *hero* as "any person admired for his or her qualities or achievements." Others say that "assuming extraordinary risk, while acting for the welfare of others"[89] qualifies one to be a hero. Although running into a flaming building is an extraordinary risk, every risk feels extraordinary for those in despair and for those with mental illnesses, and it is for the present and potential welfare of others that we live, if only to set an example. So with my limited philosophical insight, I think we are heros for "not lifting a finger."

A hero to many with mental illnesses, Patty Duke is the survivor of many suicide attempts, an abusive childhood, and manic-depressive disorder. Her autobiographical books, *Call Me Anna* and *A Brilliant Madness*, are reflections on her life, struggles, recovery efforts, and success. They are a testament to the extraordinary risks to her career and her family that she has taken in order to educate us on manic-depressive disorder.

In *Call Me Anna*, she describes her out-of-control thoughts and actions, her inability to cope with raising a family and putting dinner on the table, her crumbling marriage, and other crises. Throughout her ordeals, she saw the quiet steadfastness of her neighbor and best friend Mary Lou. "She had that kind of homespun, very basic bottom-line approach to life that really was a ground to me." Mary Lou's quiet, resolute coping and unfailing friendship was a selflessness Patty Duke had "never witnessed before."[90] For her to find a hero in her neighbor seems odd, but from her books, clearly Patty Duke knows the bravery and nobility it takes to make it through each day.

Little acts may not go unnoticed. Society may discount the heroic effort needed to survive; however, what we are going through is not easy. Give yourself credit for making it through the last five minutes, the last hour, or the last twenty-four hours. You are a hero. I applaud you.

thirty-nine

Magic

*I am sure there is Magic in everything, only we have not sense
enough to get hold of it and make it do things for us.*

—Frances Hodgson Burnett[91]

**There may not be hope right now, but something magical
or miraculous might happen any minute.**

Somehow, when I am beyond hope and faith, I come to
magic. As the magician puts the rabbit back into the hat, I
can see with my very own eyes that the rabbit has nowhere to
go. Following his wand and hearing his hocus-pocus patter
of distraction, I key in on his assistant's hands, his cape, his
cuffs, the curtain. He turns the hat inside out and the rabbit
is gone. Though I've seen the trick a dozen times, I'm still
amazed. Even knowing how the trick is done does not help
me see where the rabbit went.

Webster defines *hope* as "a desire for some good, accompa-
nied with at least a slight expectation of obtaining it, or a belief
that it is obtainable." Further, *magic*, is "any mysterious, seemingly inexplicable, or extraordinary power or influence." When
I have lost all desire for anything but relief, or any expectation
that the future holds promise, there is still a place for magic.

Magic comes from the Persian word *magus*, meaning
sorcerer. In the Christmas story of the three Magi coming to
see Jesus in Bethlehem, I find a story of magic. According to

the story, the three Magi came from Persia, following a star, or a convergence of stars, to the stable where Jesus was born. I can't imagine them riding through the vast desert on their camels, motivated only by hope. Hope alone was not strong enough to fire this extraordinary journey.

The Magi maintained their hope because of their sense of magic. Their sense of magic defied all sense of logic or folly. Carrying expensive gifts over the desert for what may have been months because of a star was beyond a traditional act of faith in God. It was beyond a desire for a savior. It was a search for the mysterious, inexplicable, and phenomenal, a search for magic. Interesting that we also call them Wise Men. Hmm...

While stuck in one of my tighter places, I read a newspaper article about smart children. Like most normal parents, I think my kids are tops so I read these stories. The reporter quoted *The Drama of the Gifted Child* by Alice Miller. Something compelled me to run out and buy the book for me or my children, I didn't know. The store had one copy in an obscure section I don't normally frequent; I wouldn't have found it by browsing. Even though I needed a dictionary to read it, the insight from this book broke a log jam for me. Her other books were easier to read, and I devoured every word as she held my hand through those pages. Finding Alice Miller was magic.

There may not be hope right now, but in the next minute, hour, day, week, or month, there might be magic. There might be a happy accident, serendipity, surprise. I might find another book, someone who finally understands me, a new friend, an old friend, a fairy godmother. Until then, what looks like folly may be wisdom in disguise. Am I wise enough to believe in magic?

forty

William Styron

But never let it be doubted that depression, in its extreme form, is madness.

—William Styron[92]

Author William Styron is a hero to me and those who survive severe depression and suicidal thoughts.

William Styron is my hero. He is the Pulitzer Prize-winning author of such classics as *Sophie's Choice* and *The Confessions of Nat Turner.* In *Darkness Visible,* he writes of his descent into the abyss of depression and suicidal thoughts and his climb out. His story rings with compassion and resolution. His story is one of hope. When I have been unable to hope, I have borrowed his. He writes: "It is hopelessness even more than pain that crushes the soul."

When my brain is so thick I can't think, it is reassuring to note that Styron, a master of words, found it difficult to describe his condition to his wife, friends, and doctor. He writes, "To most of those who have experienced it, the horror of depression is so overwhelming as to be quite beyond expression."[93]

There is comfort knowing that even a man of his skills had trouble communicating his feelings to others. I am not alone in wondering if anyone could understand this pain; or if they did, could do anything about it. How does one describe the blur? How does one harness the tornado of feelings into words? Our language doesn't have enough words or the right words to describe this state.

Drawing on "some last gleam of sanity," Styron describes how he finally called his psychiatrist and checked himself into the hospital. His doctor recommended hospitalization reluctantly, fearing that Styron would be stigmatized. Styron couldn't believe that society, especially the psychiatric profession, wasn't beyond the issue of stigma. "The hospital (and, of course, I am speaking of the many good ones)," he states, "should be shorn of its menacing reputation." In his darkest days, the hospital was a great refuge, "a place where patients still may go when pills fail."[94]

For those who can't imagine it, the book creates an image of the "despair beyond despair," and it provides hope for those who can't imagine the future. For those in the abyss, this book is a solace. Here is someone who has been there and come back in one piece. He took on the hero's journey and returned to tell us about it. The book comforts in its depiction of depression as an illness as "democratic as a Norman Rockwell poster."

Most pervasively, the book exudes hope. "If depression had no termination," Styron concludes, "then suicide would, indeed, be the only remedy. But one need not sound the false or inspirational note to stress the truth that depression is not the soul's annihilation; men and women who have recovered from the disease—and they are countless—bear witness to what is probably its only saving grace: it is conquerable."[95]

forty-one

Recovery

I have learned that success is to be measured not so much by the position that one has reached in life as by the obstacles which one has overcome while trying to succeed.

—Booker T. Washington

The highest priority is survival, not the overwhelming details of life.

At times, a day on which I felt decent was long in coming. On these good days, I would gulp in life like a camel at an oasis. During this momentary surge of strength, I would open my eyes to see the dust, the piles of unopened mail, the unpaid bills, the unreturned phone calls, the baskets of dirty clothes, and an empty refrigerator.

I would attack projects as if this might be the last productive day of my life. Inevitably, I exhausted myself and vowed I would spend the next day I felt good at the beach (even if it was 25 degrees). When that next good day came, I was again making up for lost time, trying to do too much. It has been difficult to give myself the time I need for emotional recovery and to give myself credit for how far I have come.

Many suicides occur after people start to get better. I understand why. When I seem to be on the rebound, the help leaves as the tough work starts. Duty done, supporters move on to other concerns after that first smile appears.

Relieved, they think everything is back to normal. As they rush out, the insurance company also reminds me that their check is not blank.

I find new disillusionment where I thought I'd find new hope. Some of those close to me may have trouble adjusting to the changes I am making: the new limits, new assertiveness, and new honesty. Some family members are afraid and ostracize me. I crave instant recovery. They crave "business as usual" and a return to the old days and old ways.

If I have a couple of decent days, my first thoughts are of quitting my medication and stopping therapy. I'm cured. However, I shouldn't discount the depth of struggle that brought me here. I would like to go back to where I was and pick up where I left off, but without understanding my weakness, I can't protect myself. Until I have explored the possible causes of my suicidal thoughts, I am vulnerable. In addition, my increased energy leaves me more vulnerable to acting on my feelings. Unfortunately, renewed energy does not always generate new stamina. Sometimes, I can only see the piles of work more clearly, and I again feel guilty and inadequate; I lose hope.

Setting small, realistic goals helps, at times. Closing my eyes to the mess works, for a while. However, the only real solace is reminding myself that recovery is a journey, not a day trip; and I am walking, not flying a jet. I need time, time to fight past the discouragement. People can disappoint me with their lack of help and understanding, but I cannot let that be a reflection on me. No one asks how long it took to build Rome, but it wasn't a day. Though missing quite a few of the details, Rome and I still survive. That is the point, for now.

forty-two

E-motion

No action, whether foul or fair,
Is ever done, but it leaves somewhere
A record, written by fingers ghostly
As a blessing or a curse, and mostly
In the greater weakness or greater strength
Of the acts which follow it.
  —Henry Wadsworth Longfellow[96]

Sometimes what I do to make myself feel better makes me feel worse.

When I can't even muster a sigh, others are all too ready to suggest things for me to do, such as exercise, a massage, or sex. Most experts view physical activity as a "mood elevator," a tension reliever, or at least a diversion. Recommendations abound to start an aerobics class or go jogging to improve my emotional outlook. Exercise is sensible advice, but activity sometimes stimulates me in ways that are not necessarily positive.

Terrified of getting my face wet, I swam regularly for two years without putting my face in the water. Doing the backstroke, a modified breaststroke, and kicking with a board, I avoided the terror that came with submerging my head. Finally, through a rebirthing experience, I connected my terror in the womb with my terror in the water. Now I see the pool through tight-fitting goggles and remind myself that I am not in murky amniotic fluid. Swimming feels better, but I'm not ready for a lake, and breathing is another story.

Releasing tension and stimulating muscles can release repressed emotions and stir up memories. In trying to stuff these back down, I may feel an anxiety worse than before I started. Many people sleep better after exercise, but it does not seem to help my insomnia. The result is feeling even more tired; then I chastise myself for not working out hard enough or long enough. I keep trying, though some days, my only exercise is hauling the gym bag from the house to the car, and researchers haven't found much good in that.

Sexual activity, for many, also releases tension and fosters relaxation. However, for survivors of sexual abuse, sex can heighten anxiety and guilt. Sex can elicit flashbacks of earlier abuse that leave survivors feeling emotionally exhausted rather than uplifted. An abuse survivor writes: "Whenever I open myself to feelings of passion, the memories are right there. It's a little like opening Pandora's box."[97]

There are therapeutic techniques that purposefully stimulate emotional release from the body, such as Rolfing, Reiki, or Bioenergetics. Unlike general exercise or massage, releasing emotions in a supportive environment can allow for an integration of the experience.

Bodywork based-therapies promote an opening of the body's energy that results in the ability to feel at a higher level of intensity. "In this view, every effective therapeutic maneuver generally results in the experience of anxiety," writes Alexander Lowen in *Bioenergetics*. He continues: "Progress in therapy is marked by more feeling, more anxiety, and finally more pleasure."[98]

In my experience with bodywork and massage, I found it difficult to have people touch me. It also was difficult to separate my feelings from the feelings the therapist expected me to have. "You look really angry," a bodywork therapist said to me at an appointment. "Do you want to lie down, kick the bed, and scream?" I lay down. In kicking and screaming, though, I felt as if I were putting on a show. My real emotion, I finally figured out, was fear. When I told her, she shrugged her shoulders; apparently, there were no exercises to kick out fear.

Taking care of my body can help me feel more whole and connected. Nonetheless, I need to be aware of how an activity influences my emotional state. It is no small victory to find an activity that releases tension and lifts my spirits. On the other hand, if an activity leaves me anxious, what is my body saying? These garbled messages need sorting, and a good therapist can help.

Traumatic experiences are the poisons of my life. Determined not to be a toxic waste dump, I need to clean this contamination out in some way. I am searching for a unity of body, mind, and spirit. Isn't that the YMCA motto? Until I'm there, though, I can't kill the messenger, my body, simply because it's bringing bad news.

forty-three

Gift

We tend to dwell on measurements, but they tell us very little about the real meaning of life. For that, we must turn to things which cannot be seen or which cannot be measured, to things like honesty, integrity, the strength of conscience, the love for God, service to others, humility, wisdom.

—Jimmy Carter

Although my life looks worthless now, I am curious to discover its worth.

I don't know what it is, but I was given a gift at my birth. There is something unique about me, some reason I am on this earth. A lesson in endurance isn't the only reason I am here; I was also sent to give something. There is something life expects from me even when I can expect nothing from life. It isn't clear now and may not be for years, but I will find out in time.

Sometimes I wonder if my gift (or maybe it is my job) is to live and make lots of noise about doing so. Maybe I won't reach my prime until my grandchildren are born, or I won't know my purpose until after my death when my donated organs give someone a second chance to live. I am curious. What is the secret ingredient I add to the human stew? Of course, it's so secret not even I know, but that does not mean it isn't there.

Suicide leaves the world a poorer place. The accomplishments of Ernest Hemingway, Marilyn Monroe, Judy Garland, Sylvia Plath, Vincent Van Gogh, Jack London,

Virginia Woolf, Abbie Hoffman, Mark Rothko, or Hart Crane will always have poignancy. The work they did, the lives they tried to lead, will always have to represent the work they did not do, and the years they did not live. Suicide ended their painful lives, but in the process, they cheated us.

I am grateful for their generous gifts, but could we have expected more from them? Is it selfish to want one more Judy Garland movie, one more Van Gogh painting, one more Hemingway story? I wonder about the songs not sung, the music not written, the poems not created, and feel saddened by the artistry left unexpressed. It is as if the Grinch came and stole Christmas.

It is hard to imagine what the world would be like if all those who committed suicide had lived out their full purpose in life rather than leaving the world too soon. Denied the wealth of many human spirits, the world is a poorer place. Without all our fellow travelers, we are one step further from excellence.

forty-four

Suffering

There is only one thing that I dread: not to be worthy of my sufferings.
—Fyodor Dostoevsky

There is meaning in my suffering and I want to find it.

My father-in-law liked to tell the story of a little boy digging frantically in a pile of horse manure. "Why are you digging in there?" someone asked. The little boy responded earnestly, "Because with all this manure, there must be a pony here some place." I am convinced there must be a Clydesdale in my pile, but I haven't found her yet.

What is the meaning of suffering? If I can find no meaning to this odyssey through the dark nights of the soul, then life itself becomes meaningless. Sometimes, however, I must content myself with the search. Psychiatrist Viktor Frankl explores this question in his classic, *Man's Search for Meaning.* The book is a monument to his determination to find dignity and meaning in suffering. Imprisoned in several Nazi concentration camps during World War II, Frankl spent years enduring slave labor and horrible conditions. He witnessed suicide on a daily basis as fellow prisoners lost hope and ran into the electric fence surrounding the camp.

Frankl observed that, stripped of everything, there were still choices to make. The main choice he saw was one of attitude. "The way in which a man accepts his fate and all the suffering it entails, the way in which he takes up his cross, gives him ample opportunity—even under the most difficult circumstances—to add a deeper meaning to his life.... And this decides whether he is worthy of his sufferings or not." [99]

He concluded that as inmates they could not dwell on the unanswerable questions of "why me?" or "what did I do to deserve this?" It was more meaningful "to think of ourselves as those who were being questioned by life—daily and hourly." He continues: "Life ultimately means taking the responsibility to find the right answer to its problems and to fulfill the tasks which it constantly sets for each individual. These tasks, and therefore the meaning of life, differ from man to man, and from moment to moment." [100]

As I search for meaning in my suffering, it is helpful not to forget that others have asked the same question. Asking it in a public way is the essence of much art and literature. In the artist's search for meaning in suffering and in life, I can find solace, sustenance, and universality in my quest. My own search for meaning in suffering allows me, on a different level, to appreciate the depth of soul in the blues, the existential dramas of Beckett, the tragedies of Shakespeare, and the pathos of Michelangelo's art.

Connecting with this larger world, I find support for what feels like an all-too-solitary journey to the center of myself. The diligence, dignity, and emotional generosity of the artist remind me of the overriding nobility of the human spirit. Looking for meaning in the larger cycles of life, death, and suffering, I find it is not only raining on my umbrella, although the purpose of the rain may escape me as I stand knee-deep in mud.

forty-five

Truth and Lies

You never find yourself until you face the truth.
—Pearl Bailey[101]

___

Suicide is a lie and cover-up. I want to learn the truth of my life.

I want to learn the truth of my life because I cannot be free unless I acknowledge the past and who I am today. Remembering my past, I can learn from it. Until I have found the sources of my suffering and recognize their impact, I cannot be free from their prison. I am free when I have learned how to sort out the truth from the lies, the actions from the talk, the past from the present and my feelings from those of everybody else. No buzz saw cuts my chains, but I keep hacking away with my nail file.

The myths and lies that have kept me alive until now stand ready to kill me. The myth of normality is hardest to let go. In this story, I have told myself that I had a normal childhood, normal parents, normal experiences and that it's normal to feel so much pain that killing myself is a normal response. That was the biggest, fattest lie I ever told, and I told it to myself so many years I believed it was true.

All good lies have elements of believability to them. Mark Twain was a master of the whopper and a master of the truth. In his novel, *Tom Sawyer*, Twain writes of a boy who sees things quite clearly then uses this knowledge to his advantage. While whitewashing Aunt Polly's long fence, Tom Sawyer sold his pal on helping him by pretending he was having fun, "Does a boy get a chance to whitewash a fence every day?"[102] Tom artfully got his friends to do all the work for him and part with their treasures for the privilege. Have I been paying to spread whitewash so the Tom Sawyers of the world can sit in the shade? I almost paid for the privilege with my life.

Is it a wonder I feel confused to the point of nausea? Layers of lies need sorting out, some as old as a voice yelling, "You're driving me crazy." That is only one small warp thread in the "tangled web" and if it were the only one, it might be of little significance, but it wasn't.

In the afterword to *Making Sense of Suffering*, psychotherapist Alice Miller offers this insight: "You couldn't prevent yourself from being deceived, neglected, and abused. You had no choice but to repress the knowledge and thereby surrender your consciousness. But if you go on like that you will destroy yourself....There is no healing alternative to recognizing and facing the truth."[103] Sounding so simple, it is the work of a lifetime.

Suicide is abuse, usually a lie on top of other lies. It does not change the past, but it irrevocably robs the future. Death removes any prospect of answering vengeance with dignity. I no longer have the means to understand my suffering. I cast off any accountability, any opportunity to make amends, and to grow spiritually and creatively.

Life tests our will, our spirit, and our values and we each respond to it according to our own humanity. Give yourself time to discover your own reason for living. Allow yourself an extra day to discover your own strength, recognize your hurt, and seek the truth. Find an angel. Practice peace even when you can't find it in yourself. And go back, back, back to rediscover the love from which we came and to which we will return in due time.

Ending and Beginning

What is life? It is the flash of a firefly in the night. It is the breath of a buffalo in the wintertime. It is the little shadow which runs across the grass and loses itself in the sunset.

—Crowfoot (1890)

Many have asked, "How are you now?" I am much better, thank you. The suicidal thoughts rarely drift through my head. I am still on a small, daily dose of an antidepressant, still see my therapist regularly, and long for the day I can cut back further on both. Honestly, I couldn't write this book now; my mental index of reasons is covered with spider webs and the range of my emotions has broadened.

My next project involves assembling a book using your reasons for staying alive, your survival tactics, your stories, your heroes. If you would like to share them, please write to me in care of Zebulon Press, Box 340788, Milwaukee, WI 53234.

On your submission, please print how you wish to be identified: pseudonym, initials, first name and city, full name, etc. On a cover sheet, I will need your real name and address to go in my locked file cabinet. Be bold. Be proud of your survival. This is your story and I encourage you to put your full name on it, but I will respect your wish for privacy, especially if you do not wish to hurt somebody.

Authors of those stories selected for publication will be sent a pre-press copy of their edited work, will receive credit in print, as they have chosen to be identified, and will receive a copy of the book. All of the other submissions (without cover sheet) will be made into a volume and presented to a mental health agency for use by their clients, unless you include a self-addressed stamped envelope for returning your work.

Like animals sharing body heat by huddling against the cold, sharing our limited energies can improve our lives and the lives of others. Thank you for allowing me to share with you. I feel better, and I think you made the difference.

notes

Acknowledgments and Permissions

The author gratefully acknowledges the authors and publishers of copyrighted material used in this book. She thanks you for your wisdom, for amplifying her voice, and for helping her feel less alone. Although every effort was made to insure the completeness of these notes, errors and omissions may have occurred and will be corrected in subsequent editions.

Preface

1. *To My Daughters, With Love* by Pearl S. Buck (New York: John Day, 1967), p. 34. Copyright © 1949, 1957, 1960, 1962, 1963, 1964 by Pearl S. Buck, copyright © 1967 by The Pearl S. Buck Foundation, Inc.

2. *A General Selection from the Works of Sigmund Freud*, ed. John Rickman, MD (New York: Anchor Books, 1989), p. 133.

Chapter 2

3. *Time;* 22 November 1950.

4. Freud, p. 199. *(see note 2)*

Chapter 3

5. *The Souls of Black Folk: Essays and Sketches* by W. E. B. Du Bois (Cutchogue, New York: Buccaneer Books, 1976), pp. 16-17.

Chapter 4

6. *Mr. Rogers' Neighborhood* by Fred Rogers. Copyright © 1995 by Family Communication. Used by courtesy of the copyright holder.

Chapter 5

7. "To Whom My Hand Goes Out" in *Selected Poems* by Carl Sandburg (New York: Gramercy Books, 1992), p. 190.

Chapter 6

8. *The Unfinished Country: A Book of American Symbols* by Max Lerner (New York: Simon & Schuster, 1959), p. 203. Copyright © 1959 by Max Lerner.

9. *The Mind* by Richard Restak, MD (New York: Bantam Books, 1988), p. 191. Copyright © 1988 by Educational Broadcasting Corporation and Richard M. Restak, MD. Used by permission of the publisher.

10. *Listening to Prozac* by Peter D. Kramer (New York: Viking Press, 1993), p. 284. Copyright © 1993 by Peter D. Kramer.

Chapter 7

11. Restak, p. 176. *(see note 9)*

12. From *Annals of Internal Medicine*, 1994; vol. 121, pp. 372-376.

13. *Signet/Mosby's Medical Encyclopedia*, s.v. "serotonin."

14. *How to Feel Better and Live Longer* by Linus Pauling (New York: W. H. Freeman, 1986), pp. 19-20. Copyright © 1986 by Linus Pauling. Used by permission of Crellin Pauling.

Chapter 8

15. From *American Family Physician*, 1991; vol. 43, pp. 477-485.

16. From *Useful Information on Sleep Disorders* (a pamphlet) by Gerald S. Snyder for the National Institute of Mental Health (1987).

17. From *JAMA*, 1989; vol. 262, pp. 1479-1485.

Chapter 9

18. *The Poet at the Breakfast Table* by Oliver Wendell Holmes (Boston: Houghton, 1872).

19. From *Western Journal of Medicine*, 1994; vol. 161, p. 194.

20. From *The Lancet*, 1992; vol. 339, pp. 727-729.

21. Restak, p. 178. *(see note 9)*

22. From *American Journal of Psychiatry*, 1994; vol. 151, pp. 1605-1615.

23. "Gene Linked to Mental Illness, Suicide," by Bruce Bower in *Science News;* 15 June 1991, p. 373.

Chapter 10

24. From *JAMA*, 1990; vol. 263, pp. 3051-3056.

25. Restak, p. 106. *(see note 9)*

Chapter 11

26. *Fortitude* by Hugh Walpole (New York: George H. Doran, 1913), p. 3.

Chapter 12

27. *Death of the Heart* by Elizabeth Bowen (New York: Alfred A. Knopf, 1938). Copyright © 1938 by Elizabeth Bowen.

28. *Co-Dependence: Misunderstood—Mistreated* by Anne Wilson Schaef (New York: HarperCollins Publishers, Inc., 1986), p. 54. Copyright © 1986 by Anne Wilson Schaef.

Chapter 13

29. *The Invisible Man* by Ralph Ellison (New York: Random House, 1952). Copyright © 1947, 1948, 1952 by Ralph Ellison.

Chapter 14

30. *Milwaukee Sentinel;* 3 June 1983: sec. A, 1.

31. *The Power of Myth* by Joseph Campbell (New York: Doubleday, 1988), p. 110. Copyright © 1988 by Apostrophe S Productions and Alfred van der Marck Editions. Used by permission of the publisher.

Chapter 15

32. *The American Way of Death* by Jessica Mitford (New York: Simon & Schuster, 1963), p. 16. Copyright © 1963 by Jessica Mitford.

Chapter 16

33. *Escape from Evil* by Ernest Becker (New York: The Free Press, 1975), p. 49. Copyright © 1975 by Marie Becker.

Chapter 17

34. *The Observer;* 8 April 1979.

35. *Phaedo* by Plato: 62.

36. *Summa Theologica* by Thomas Aquinas (London: Blackfriars Press, 1966), Part II-II, Question 64:5.

37. "The Doctine of Virtue," Part II of *The Metaphysics of Morals* by Immanuel Kant, translated by Mary J. Gregor (Philadelphia: University of Pennsylvania Press, 1964), p. 85. Copyright © 1964 by Mary J. Gregor.

38. From *Ethics* by Dietrich Bonhoeffer, translated from the German by Neville Horton Smith (New York: The Macmillan Company, 1955), pp. 168, 170. Copyright © 1955 by The Macmillan Company, New York. All rights reserved. Used by permission of the publisher.

39. *Principles of Biomedical Ethics,* 4th ed. by Tom L. Beauchamp and James F. Childress (New York: Oxford University Press, 1994), p. 62, 286. Copyright © 1979, 1983, 1989, 1994 by Oxford University Press, Inc.

Chapter 18

40. *Atlas Shrugged* by Ayn Rand (New York: Random House, 1957). Copyright © 1957 by Ayn Rand.

Chapter 19

41. *The Drama of the Gifted Child*, by Alice Miller, translated by Ruth Ward (New York: Basic Books, 1981), p. 58. Copyright © 1979 by Suhrkamp Verlag, Frankfurt am Main, Germany.

42. *May Sarton: A Self-Portrait* by May Sarton, ed. Marita Simpson and Martha Wheelock (New York: W. W. Norton & Company, 1982), p. 35. Copyright © 1982 by Marita Simpson, Martha Wheelock, and Ishtar Enterprises. Used by permission of the publisher.

Chapter 20

43. *Miss Manners' Guide to the Turn of the Millennium* by Judith Martin (New York: Pharos Press, 1989), p. 121. Copyright © 1989 by United Feature Syndicate, Inc.

Chapter 21

44. From *American Journal of Obstetrics and Gynecology*, 1989; vol. 161, pp. 1228-1235.

45. From *American Journal of Psychiatry*, 1989; vol. 146, pp. 829-840.

46. *Toxic Metal Syndrome* by H. Richard Casdorph and Morton Walker (Garden City Park, New York: Avery Publishing Group, 1995), p. 73. Copyright © 1995 by H. Richard Casdorph and Morton Walker.

47. From *The Lancet*, 1994; vol. 343, pp. 1150-1151.

48. From *Archives of Internal Medicine*, 1995; vol. 155, pp. 262-269.

Chapter 22

49. *Orthodoxy* by G. K. Chesterton (New York: Image Books, 1959), p. 40. Copyright © 1908, 1936 by Dodd, Mead & Company.

50. *Waiting for Godot* by Samuel Beckett (New York: Grove Press, 1954), p. 60. Copyright © 1954 by Grove Press. Used by permission.

Chapter 23

51. *A Christmas Carol in Prose: Being a Ghost Story of Christmas* by Charles Dickens (New York: Atheneum, 1966), p. 33.

52. Dickens, p. 27.

53. *The Unquiet Dead* by Edith Fiore (New York: Doubleday, 1987), p. 37. Copyright © 1987 by Edith Fiore. Used by permission of the publisher.

54. Fiore, p. 117.

55. Dickens, p. 31.

Chapter 24

56. *Hassan* by James Elroy Flecker (New York: Alfred A. Knopf, 1924), p. 162.

57. *Coming Back to Life* by P. M. H. Atwater (New York: Ballantine Books, 1988), pp. 19-20. Copyright © 1988 by P. M. H. Atwater. Used by permission of the author.

58. Atwater, p. 17.

59. *Beyond the Darkness: My Near-Death Journey to the Edge of Hell and Back* by Angie Fenimore (New York: Bantam Books, 1995), p. 146. Copyright © 1995 by Angie Fenimore.

60. *Beyond the Light: What Isn't Being Said About the Near-Death Experience* by P. M. H. Atwater (Secaucus, New Jersey: Birch Lane Press, 1994), p. 17. Copyright © 1994 by P. M. H. Atwater.

61. *Reflections on Life after Life* by Raymond A. Moody, Jr. MD (Harrisburg, Pennsylvania: Stackpole Books, 1977), p. 41. Copyright © 1977 by Dr. Raymond A. Moody, Jr.

Chapter 25

62. *Out of the Trap: Selected Lectures of Alan W. Watts* by Alan W. Watts, ed. Mark Watts (South Bend, Indiana: And Books, 1985), p. 61. Copyright © 1985 by Mark Watts.

63. Freud, p. 158. *(see note 2)*

64. *The Way of Karma* by Charles Breaux (York Beach, Maine: Samuel Weiser, 1993), p. 6. Copyright © 1993 by Charles Breaux.

Chapter 26

65. Sarton, p. 23. *(see note 42)*

66. *The Enigma of Suicide* by George Howe Colt (New York: Summit Books, 1991), p. 81. Copyright © 1991 by George Howe Colt.

Chapter 27

67. Description from Du Bois, *Souls,* ch. XIV. *(see note 5)*

68. Colt, p. 453.

Chapter 28

69. "The Long Search for Pride" by Gordon Parks in *Life;* 16 August 1963.

70. "Coping with a Co-Worker's Suicide" by Mary McGlothin Davis in *Personnel Journal,* June 1990; vol. 69, pp. 40-47. Copyright © 1990 by *Personnel Journal.* Used by permission.

71. Excerpt from "Living with Chronic Illness" by Stephen Schmidt. Copyright © 1989 Christian Century Foundation. Reprinted by permission from the May 3, 1989 issue of *The Christian Century*.

Chapter 29

72. *The Magic Mountain* by Thomas Mann, translated from the German by H. T. Lowe-Porter (New York: Alfred A. Knopf, 1975). Copyright © 1927 by Alfred A. Knopf, copyright © 1952 by Thomas Mann.

Chapter 30

73. *The Complete Poems of Emily Dickinson*, ed. Thomas H. Johnson (Boston: Little, Brown & Company, 1960), # 1765.

74. Freud, p. 14. *(see note 2)*

Chapter 32

75. "A Fight to the Death" by Trip Gabriel in *The New York Times Magazine;* 8 December 1991, p. 46. Copyright © 1991 by The New York Times Company. Used by permission of the publisher.

76. Gabriel, p. 88.

Chapter 33

77. "The Octopus File," by Phil Linsalata in the *Columbia Journalism Review,* vol. 30, issue 4, p. 78. Copyright © November 1991 by the *Columbia Journalism Review*. Used by permission of the publisher.

78. Linsalata, p. 76.

Chapter 34

79. *The Wit and Wisdom of the 20th Century,* ed. Frank S. Pepper (New York: Peter Bedrick Books, 1987), p. 130. Copyright © 1987 by Frank S. Pepper.

80. *When the State Kills ... The Death Penalty: A Human Rights Issue* (London: Amnesty International Publications, 1989).

Chapter 35

81. *Treasure Island* by Robert Louis Stevenson (New York: Grossett & Dunlap, 1947), pp. 249-250.

Chapter 36

82. *Sisters of the Earth,* ed. by Lorraine Anderson (New York: Vintage Books, 1991), pp. 100-101. Compilation copyright © 1991 by Lorraine Anderson.

83.   *The Power of Your Other Hand: A Course in Channeling the Inner Wisdom of the Right Brain* by Lucia Capaccione (North Hollywood, California: Newcastle Publishing, 1988).

84.   *For Your Own Good: Hidden Cruelty in Child-Rearing and the Roots of Violence* by Alice Miller, translated by Hildegarde and Hunter Hannun (New York: Farrar, Straus & Giroux, Inc., 1983), p. 242. Copyright © 1983 by Alice Miller.

Chapter 37

85.   Five lines from "It's Possible" from *Selected Poems of Rainer Maria Rilke,* edited and translated by Robert Bly (New York: Harper and Row, 1981), p. 55. Copyright © 1981 by Robert Bly. Reprinted by permission of HarperCollins Publishers, Inc.

86.   *Marilyn: Norma Jeane* by Gloria Steinem (New York: Henry Holt & Company, 1987), p. 31. Copyright © 1987 by East Toledo Productions, Inc. Reprinted by permission of the publisher.

87.   Steinem, p. 28.

Chapter 38

88.   *Journal* by Henry David Thoreau (New York: Houghton Mifflin, 1906).

89.   Beauchamp and Childress, p. 497. *(see note 39)*

90.   *Call Me Anna: The Autobiography of Patty Duke* by Patty Duke and Kenneth Turan (New York: Bantam Books, 1987), p. 303. Copyright © 1987 by Patty Duke.

Chapter 39

91.   *The Secret Garden* by Frances Hodgson Burnett (New York: Alfred A. Knopf, 1988), p. 177.

Chapter 40

92.   Excerpt from *Darkness Visible: A Memoir of Madness* by William Styron (New York: Random House, 1990), p. 46. Copyright © 1990 by William Styron. Reprinted by permission of the publisher.

93.   Styron, pp. 62, 83.

94.   Styron, pp. 67, 68, 72.

95.   Styron, pp. 35, 84.

Chapter 42

96.   *Christus: The Golden Legend* by Henry Wadsworth Longfellow (Boston: James R. Osgood, 1872): part III.

97. *The Courage to Heal* by Ellen Bass and Laura Davis (New York: Harper & Row, 1988), p. 255. Copyright © 1988 by Ellen Bass and Laura Davis.

98. *Bioenergetics* by Alexander Lowen, MD (New York: Putnam-Berkley Group, 1975), p. 129. Copyright © 1975 by Alexander Lowen, MD. Reprinted by permission of the publisher.

Chapter 44

99. From *Man's Search for Meaning* by Viktor E. Frankl (Boston: Beacon Press), p. 76. Copyright © 1959, 1962, 1984, 1992 by Viktor E. Frankl. Reprinted by permission of Beacon Press, Boston.

100. Frankl, p. 77.

Chapter 45

101. *The Raw Pearl* by Pearl Bailey (New York: Harcourt, Brace & World, 1968), p. 202. Copyright © 1968 by Pearl Bailey.

102. *The Adventures of Tom Sawyer* by Mark Twain (New York: Wm. Morrow, 1989), p. 14.

103. *Making Sense of Suffering* by J. Konrad Stettbacher, foreword and afterword by Alice Miller, translated by Simon Worrall (New York: Dutton-Penguin Books), p. 123. English translation copyright © 1991 by J. Konrad Stettbacher. Foreword and afterword copyright © 1991 by Alice Miller.